QUADERNI DI ARABIA ANTICA 4

Alexia Pavan
Michele Degli Esposti

The urban shrine in Quarter A at Sumhuram

Stratigraphy, Architecture, Material Culture

«L'ERMA» di BRETSCHNEIDER

Quaderni di Arabia Antica 4
series directed by Alessandra Avanzini

Alexia Pavan, Michele degli Esposti
The urban shrine in Quarter A at Sumhuram.
Stratigraphy, architecture, material culture

Editing, page layout and cover: Alessandra Lombardi
English text editor: Evan M. Rap

Pavan Alexia, Degli Esposti Michele,
The urban shrine in Quarter A at Sumhuram. Stratigraphy, architecture, material culture / Alexia Pavan, Michele Degli Esposti - Roma : «L'ERMA» di BRETSCHNEIDER 2016.
- 60 p. + 31 tavole : ill ; 21 cm. (Quaderni di Arabia Antica ; 4)

ISBN: 978-88-913-1141-2 (paperback)
ISBN: 978-88-913-1147-4 (digital edition)

CDD 953.91
1. Archeologia - Arabia

Index

1. Introduction

In February 2008 a new urban shrine was discovered in the ancient South Arabian town of Sumhuram (Fig. 1). Its original layout comprised a small main room (A110) linked with a smaller, ancillary room to the north (A152), whose excavation was completed in 2010. Decisive evidence was found to identify a real urban shrine, smaller but in a remarkably central position if compared with the already known temple of Sīn in Area F (Sedov 2008a). The shrine is in fact located in the so-called Area A, south of the massive building named Monumental Building 1 (Fig. 2).
The stratigraphy revealed within the shrine, reaching down to the earliest levels of the city, clearly indicates two main periods of occupation each comprising several sub-phases, finally followed by a late, more ephemeral occupation.

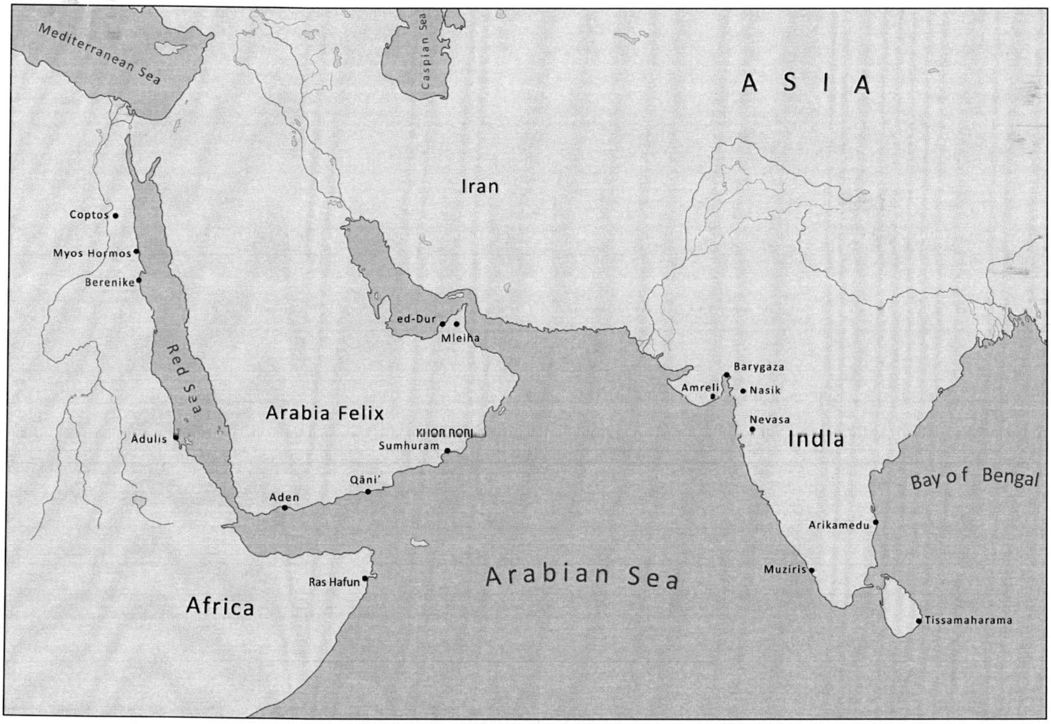

FIGURE 1. *The location of Sumhuram along the coast of South Arabia, and the main sites involved in the Indian Ocean trade (map by A. Lombardi).*

FIGURE 2. *General plan of the city showing the different areas of excavation (Area A, B, F). 1: the urban shrine; 2: temple of Sīn; 3: so-called Monumental Building 1 (hosting the well); 4: so-called Monumental Building 2 (plan A. Massa and S. Rossi).*

This stratigraphic and chronological sequence can be used as a reference for the general revision work of the other excavated areas still in progress. It also mirrors the broad phasing that has been more recently proposed for the city as a whole and confirms the recent re-assessment of the chronology made by Alessandra Avanzini (2014).

Moreover, its excavation presented an assemblage that, though being quite common in terms of general typologies of the objects, is nevertheless noteworthy due to the stylistic peculiarities of the artefacts. A first discussion of these objects is presented here.

2. The excavation: stratigraphy and architectural evolution

Period 1 (Phases I-IV)

The building originally comprised two adjacent rooms, A110 and A152, with access to the shrine (A110), from a door placed in its eastern wall (Fig. 3).

A110, the actual shrine, was trapezoidal in shape, east-west oriented, and roughly 4.5x4.8 meters wide. Its pavement, US417floor, stood at the average elevation of 27.75 m a.s.l. Perimeter walls, clockwise from north, were M404+M402, M403, M248 and M290. On the northern side a second door, dividing M402 from M404, lead to a little rectangular premise (A152), only 1.2x2.2 m wide. Other walls of its perimeter were, clockwise, M274, M400 and M270 (Fig. 4, Plate 1). The original pavement of room A152 was US431floor, well plastered and standing at an elevation of 27.94 meters a.s.l. This floor was removed in ancient times to leave room to a slightly higher one.[1] In the main room, US417floor was well preserved and randomly scattered with circular reddish spots of hardened plaster that could represent the lighting of small open fires inside the building. This floor was characterized by a remarkable thickness, over 35.0 cm, which accounts for the slight difference in height between it and the adjacent part of the quarter excavated east of the shrine. A few rough stones were visible set within the mortar; a bronze coin (Co643) was retrieved while removing the upper portion of this floor.

The main entrance showed no peculiar feature apart from a low threshold. Conversely, the door linking the two rooms was marked by a low step and still bears traces of plaster on its uprights which indicate the position of the door wing. Plaster also defined a narrow raised ridge across the threshold. While the northern room seems to be nothing but an empty ancillary room, which also presented no significant finds, the main room had a complex internal layout. Immediately left of the entrance a one-flight stair of which only four steps survive (M435) was set against the eastern wall M290, also abutting against wall M404 (western part of the northern wall). This clearly indicates the existence of an upper storey or, at least, an accessible roof, of which no direct trace remains. Low stone benches ran along the northern (bench M445), the eastern (bench M446) and the western (bench M448) walls. Bench M445 must have ended in correspondence with the door leading to room A152, though its later additional portion was not removed during excavation: this reconstruction is confirmed by the limits of the original plastering on its top.

---

[1] A sounding dug in a small portion of the room showed that floor US431floor was resting directly above a layer of quite compact loam with medium size stones at its base and small stone flecks interspersed within it, something similar to the widespread "foundation filling" defined in many locales throughout the city, laid down as a setting for all the first phase buildings.

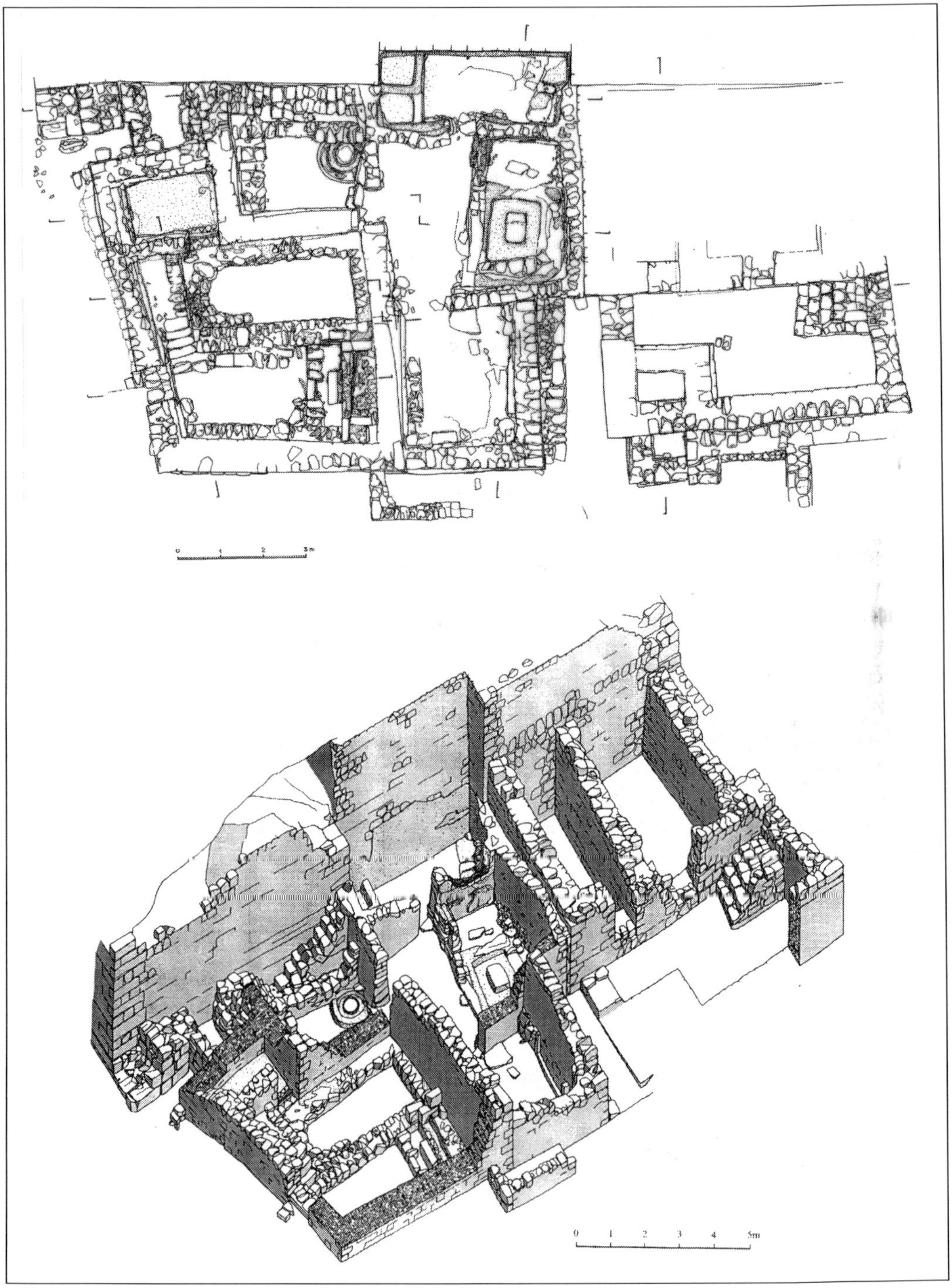

FIGURE 3. *Detailed plan and axonometric view of the shrine (Period 1) and adjacent area, immediately south of the Monumental Building 1 (drawings by E. Kurkina).*

All of these benches comprised one or two courses of rough stones embedded in clay, with their smoothest side facing the interior of the room. A thin layer of plaster covered them all over the top and the face, in continuity with the floor.
Another low wall, consisting of two parallel rows of stones one course high, M447, crossed the room east to west, aligned with the stairs base and thus bisecting the room. Although M447 closely resembles the perimeter benches, its function must have been different. In fact, given the dimensions of the room, a central support for the roof was necessary, and evidence for its presence was collected and associated with Period 2 (see below). M447 can thus be interpreted as a basement primarily meant to host the wooden pillars supporting the roof structure, a rather common feature within Ḥaḍrami architecture.[2] Its plastering suggests that it also served other purposes: seating place during ceremonies, or stand for cultic furnishing. That a complete wooden wall, or hanging mats or curtains, separated the southern and northern halves of the shrine cannot be ruled out.
Be that as it may, the southern part of the shrine – likely the real *cella* – hosted the prominent feature of this phase, the C-shaped altar M449 (Fig. 4). Abutting the eastern wall, it was severely disturbed by later works which involved its partial dismantling. Two quadrangular structures,

FIGURE 4. *General view of the shrine, Phase I, from the west.*

---

[2] The same feature occurred also in the *extra muros* temple at Sumhuram where the benches were used as foundations for possibly wooden pillars supporting the roof (Sedov 2005a; Pavan and Sedov 2008).

possibly small tanks, stood at its sides (the northern actually very badly preserved). The altar was built using squared sandstone blocks for its sides, while the rear and the bottom parts were probably all built of rough limestone blocks bounded and covered with mortar, like the altar of Period 2 (see below).

M451, one course of stones high (about 0.2 m) and including reused blocks, was later added to the area around the altar (Plate 2). Meant to frame two new cultic features, it also served as a stepped access to the altar. A squared limestone block, placed on top of M451 between the two cultic features, formed a second step; it is possible that the block was actually removed from the altar and dislocated in the new position with a new function (Fig. 5).

Of the two new cultic features, the one to the north was a small rectangular plaster tank. No outstanding deposits were associated with this feature which could provide any indication of its function. Although a use connected with water-based rituals cannot be excluded, it seems more plausible that it was meant to host a removable feature, like a mobile water basin or an incense burner. To the opposite side of the central step, against bench M448, a 35 cm deep, oval pit (US420) was dug through the plaster of the original floor US417. It was found filled with ashes and charcoal (US430). It was also likely meant to host some removable feature, possibly in bronze, as suggested by a small piece of this metal retrieved stuck at its bottom.

Quite soon a new plaster floor, US403 (2.0/3.0 cm thick), was laid down in A152 above a thick gravel preparation layer (US431), after dismantling US431floor. On top of US403 a couple of fired spots were visible, similar to those found in room A110.

FIGURE 5. *General view of the shrine, Phase III, from the west.*

A new construction phase is indicated by the earthen floor US416, laid down in the main room. Benches were enlarged with the addition of M444 in the northern half of the room and of the poorly made M443 in the southern half; a short segment of bench was possibly added in the southwest corner as well (Plate 3).
Several stones were reused in the construction of M443, of which two deserve mention: a long, rectangular, broken offering table placed face down on the floor (S1538, see cat. 7), and a limestone pillar with a raised decoration representing a snake (S1539, cat. 19).
Other significant finds collected from US416 are a displaced architectural element decorated with the usual motif of the solar disk and moon crescent (S1532, cat. 21) and a coin issued by Yashhur'il Yuhar'ish, son of Abīyasa', mukarrib of Ḥaḍramawt (Co628). A few beads in different materials (S1509, S1526, G142, Sh358; cat. 41-44) were found as well.
During the last phase of Period 1 (sub-phase IV) the layout of the shrine changed substantially (Plate 4). The floor level was raised by means of layer of brown loam – US416 (25.0 to 30.0 cm thick) – in turn serving as a base for the new plaster floor US406, thinner than the others and poorly preserved. The average elevation of floor US406 is 28.09 m a.s.l., meaning that the gap between the floors in the main room and A152 was now filled (Plate 12). All the internal features of room A110 were thus buried beneath the floor, with the exception of the altar and the stairs. It is likely that supporting posts were still in use, although no evidence of their housings was visible on US416. Possibly in this phase the basin located south of the altar was split in two by the placement of a reused architectural element.
Towards the end of Period 1 the passage leading to room A152 was closed with M423, erected at the same pace with the filling up of this little room. Its southern face shows that it was erected before the deposition of the collapse layer US405 (see below), and remained visible (Fig. 6). Since the stairs continued to be in use, it is possible that this filling was meant to strengthen and expand the second floor, with room A152 turned into a sort of compartmented basement.[3]

Fig. 6. The door leading to room A152 completely walled up by wall M23, seen form the south (left); and from inside room A152 (right).

---

[3] There is evidence, from a series of premises unearthed between the shrine and the Monumental Building 1 (in course of study by the authors), that in a late moment of the first period of the city's existence, there could be a system of second floor little platforms, one of which could actually be located on top of former room A152.

Room A152 was backfilled by means of two superimposed thick layers, US403 and US396. The former, laid down directly above the room's plaster floor, had a crumbly loam texture, dark brown in colour, with the presence of small stones and gravels. Abundant charcoal and animal bones were found in this layer. In the north eastern part of the room an ash lens was identified, directly resting on the underlying surface US431floor, likely the outcome of waste throwing before carrying on the filling up of the premise. Above US403, the quite loose, lighter brown loam layer US396 was identified, characterized by the remarkable quantity of crumbled mudbricks.

The collapse of the first shrine

Floor US406 lay under a thick sequence of layers connected with (accidental?) destruction and deliberate deposition of loam and debris (Fig. 7). Their layout indicates that the reason for the massive re-arrangement of the shrine was the collapse of part of the first and of the second floor (or roof) of the building. Directly above floor US406 stood in fact US405, a layer comprising a remarkable quantity of plaster fragments, ashes and charcoal. This layer mostly accumulated against the south-eastern corner, where the altar stood: here the fragments of plaster were retrieved, chaotically collapsed and mixed with ashes. Several of them bore traces on the back side indicating their original use as a wall's sheathing.

Ashes and charcoal were more abundant slightly north of this debris layer, where they included some fragmentary objects and pottery sherds. There was enough charcoal to provide a suitable sample for radiocarbon dating, which gave back a 2σ calibrated date ranging 106 BC – 71 AD[4] (see Fig. 30a).

US405 was further sealed under a massive layer of loam and mud-bricks lumps (US394, see Plate 5). There is evidence for bricks realized using both grey and brown clay, as already noticed for walls in other parts of the city. The presence of these mudbricks could tentatively be linked to their application on the upper part of the walls, possibly levelled to allow reconstruction after collapse; admittedly, there is little evidence to safely support this hypothesis. US394 completely filled up the room, and much of its loam had to be intentionally carried in from elsewhere in order to complete the levelling. It thus served as a base for the reconstruction of Period 2's shrine. Noteworthy was the absence of traces connected to collapsed wooden beams, which had to constitute the main frame of the roof or upper floor pavement, although it is possible that the sound ones were reused. A bronze coin of Ilīʿazz was found in this layer (Co630), together with several objects, including the incense burners S1503 and S1504 (cat. 11-12), the mortar S1518 (cat. 28), and the fragmentary bronze handle MB626 (cat. 33). A collection of quartz game dices (S1537, cat. 51) could also possibly be linked with some ritual purpose, as well as the bead S1535 (cat. 47). Stone elements S1540 and S1514 should be included in the architectural decoration of the shrine: S1540 (cat. 25) was re-employed in the plaster tank near wall M449, while S1514 (cat. 24) was a decorative element. The typical motif of the false window visible on S1514 strongly supports the interpretation as an architectural element and finds parallel in specimens coming from the necropolis of Timnaʿ (Cleveland 1965: 139, pl. 95).

---

[4] Lab. Code: 14Fi 1574; 14Fi 1577.

FIGURE 7. *A view of Period 2's altar resting on earlier deposits (top) and the stratigraphy connected to Period 1's last phase and to the shrine's collapse (bottom).*

The sequence laid out above not only indicates that the building underwent a severe collapse and was then rebuilt at a higher elevation, but also supplies evidence that this collapse mainly affected the eastern part of the building and was likely linked with a fire which started there, as indicated by the concentration of ashes and charcoal. That this was the case can be further supported by the severe damage visible in wall M403 and its corner with the wall M402. These walls were partially rebuilt from the outside (Fig. 8), where the occupation levels were probably kept to a lower height for a longer time. Furthermore, in the corner between them, above US405, a big stone was laid inside an appositely created pit and then backfilled with loose grey clay of the same kind used for mudbricks. This stone was clearly placed to provide more strength to the damaged corner, which will be further strengthen in Period 2 with the erection of structure M409 (see below).

The location of the plaster fragments and the few objects retrieved from amongst them suggest that the importance of the altar was enhanced by the presence of plastered walls in the corresponding corner. The retrieval of a bronze half-relief lion, MB625 (Fig. 9, see cat. 4), still attached to its plaster background, points to a use that is usually associated with inscribed plaques, i.e., the suspension on shrines and temples walls. The same function could then be hypothesized for the full-relief limestone snake S1529 (cat. 3), recovered from the same layer together with other small finds connected with the preparation and the cooking of different items (see the mortars S1507, S1522 and the stone vessels S1505 and S1508). Glass (G140, G141, cat. 45-46)

FIGURE 8. *The rebuilt northern portion of M403 seen from the northeast (1, the arrow indicates the gap between the later and the original part) and the corner between M402 and M403, where a wooden post was possibly placed (2).*

FIGURE 9. *The bronze lion applique MB625 at the moment of its discovery, with walls' plaster still stuck on its back.*

and stone (S1501, cat. 48) beads were also discovered, as well as small utilitarian metal tools (MI159 and MI160, cat. 35-36). A fragmentary stone artifact shaped as an animal foot, possibly an architectural element, also came from this layer (S1519, cat. 23).

Period 2 (Phases V-IX)

During the first phases of Period 2, room A110 maintained the same perimeter (Plate 5). A new threshold made up of rough stones bound with clay and with a shallow step on both sides of the door was built for the entrance.[5] A new C-shaped altar was placed in the same corner of the room but was now oriented northward and placed against M248. Like the earlier structure, it was created out of squared rectangular sandstone blocks on both sides, and more irregular blocks or rough stones in the rear (Fig. 10). One of the reused blocks was S1531 (cat. 20), a decorated limestone block similar to S1532 mentioned above, and probably also from the original altar M449. The altar base was built with undressed stones, laid down in and covered with mortar up to a height of 18 cm above the floor. Its sides and back reached a height of 85.0 cm. In front of the altar, placed against the north-eastern corner of the room, stood a cubic mudbrick structure (M409), made up of grey clay mudbricks bound with a brown clay mortar, providing the structure with a remarkable strength and compactness (Fig. 11). On top of this feature stood a shallow recess marked by an irregular rough stones frame, probably meant to host some removable temple furniture. The first plaster floor of the renewed shrine was US391, a badly preserved, thin (1.0 cm) plaster layer with an average elevation of 28.62 m a.s.l. It sat directly on top of the fillings which obliterated Period 1 remains. This plaster is also connected with the wall plaster still visible on the south-eastern corner of the room, between M248 and M403.

---

[5] The elevation of street A80 had been obviously also raised: several occupational levels are discernible within the stratigraphy accumulated on the road, of which a thorough study is due.

FIGURE 10. *Frontal view of Period 2's altar, M419, in its original layout. The whiter stone in the middle of the rear part is S1532.*

FIGURE 11. *The "basin" standing on top of the cubic feature M409.*

During Period 2 the shrine was continuously rearranged and gradually endowed with features mirroring those of Period 1, while the floors were constantly restored and raised.
US390floor, above US391, marked the first re-arrangement (Plate 6). New benches were built all around the perimeter (M411 to M414 clockwise from west), using the same technique as those of Period 1, with their footings incorporated in the plaster floor. This was a well laid, compact layer of lime-base plaster comprising gravel and rare pottery fragments used as temper. The only exception was M413, whose lower course was realized using clay-bound grey mudbricks as for M409 (Fig. 12).
A new mudbrick feature, M417, was erected in the corner between the altar and M403, again using clay-bound grey mudbricks. It probably hosted on its top another tank or recess. The altar was also slightly modified by the addition of a dressed and polished limestone block (S1533, cat. 22) placed against the front of its base and set in the floor's plaster (Fig. 13). Its upper edge

FIGURE 12. *Detail of bench M413's structure showing the use of grey mud bricks bound with brown clay. The same materials were employed in the construction of coeval benches and of the cubic feature M409.*

FIGURE 13. *Detail of the dressed stone placed to block the frontal part of the altar during Phase VI.*

showed evident fractures, hidden by plaster: all points to a late reuse of what was probably a lintel belonging to an earlier building. This stone was narrower than the altar, the voids beings filled with further mortar. The latter also linked the altar with the eastern bench, on the one hand, and with M416 on the other. This new feature was a rectangular low hump covered by US390 plaster and made up of grey mudbricks bound with clay, whose function is unclear. It ran from the altar's western stem towards the opposite side of the room, ending in alignment with bench M414 but also with the new, squared pillar M418. This comprised a base of undressed stones englobed in US390floor and surmounted by a dressed, parallelepiped sandstone, all bound with mortar. That this pillar was part of the cult taking place in the room is made evident by the presence of four holes in the floor between the pillar and the altar (Fig. 14): traces of bronze retrieved in two of the holes suggest that this could be the place for some kind of removable bronze altar/offering table, easily removed when the room was modified and later abandoned. Floor US390 also lined a hollow pit located between bench M413 and the altar. No evidence for its use was collected, but its importance in the activities of the shrine was shown by the presence of similar features in the following phases (Fig. 15).

This sub-phase came to an end when a 7.0 to 12.0 cm thick layer of brown soil, medium compact with very few materials included (US390), was laid down as a base for the new plaster floor US389. The latter thus reached the same elevation of the lower step of the threshold (Plate 7). The new floor, 2.0 cm thick, differs slightly from the previous ones in that it contains a higher rate of gravels, thus presenting a more uneven appearance. Directly above the floor a silver coin of ʿAmdān Bayyin, king of Saba' and dhū-Raydān (Co616) was found. It was associated with US389, though it is actually linked to the moment when a further floor (US388, see below) was laid down. Near the north-western corner of the room, US389 showed a wide lacuna, leaving the remains of underlying floor US390 visible: this showed how one of the reasons for repeated re-paving was the settling of the conspicuous amount of loam and mudbrick lumps covering Period 1 ruins.

Apart from rearrangements of the internal layout, one feature deserves mention due to its structural implication. Almost in the middle of the room, a wooden post was set inside a post pit cut through the previous floor (pit US395). At its bottom, a large flat stone was placed to sustain the post, subsequently surrounded by US390 and US389, so that on top of floor US389 the pit's shape corresponds to the diameter of the post.

In front of the altar, a rectangular space was created by the addition of various features. Bench M420 was built against M409 southern face and linked to the eastern bench M414. At its western end it was also linked to another new bench, M415, built on top of M416. Both the new benches were made up of rough stones (both lime- and sandstone) bound with plaster and were also plastered on the top and on the sides. A second pillar, M421, was placed between M418 and the altar, where the removable offering table previously stood. It was made of irregular stones set in mortar, sitting on top of floor US390, and topped by an undressed, irregularly circular limestone block (Fig. 16).

This rectangular area was covered by yet another layer of compact plaster, US392, which defined a sort of hollow channel all around the two pillars and completely hid the dressed stone in front of the altar. US392 actually merged with US389, and both bench M415 and the altar were encased in plaster. A second plastered pit was also placed against the altar and adjacent to the previous one.

The renewal of plaster surfaces continued, albeit only in certain places and mainly in front of the altar, until floor US388 was laid down in the room (Plate 8). Its quality was clearly worse

FIGURE 14. *The area in front of the altar in Phase VI, seen from the south: the possible housings of a removable bronze altar are visible in the floor plaster.*

FIGURE 15. *General view of the shrine, Phase VI, from the west. The central pit is an intrusive feature from later phases.*

than the preceding ones: it was made of compact brown-greyish loam, intermixed with mostly pulverized mortar that offered good compactness. This floor stood at the same elevation as the entrance threshold.

Of the two pits on the western side of the altar, only the northern one survived, though partially filled by US388 itself. The other was completely backfilled with loose mortar and loam, and sealed with a 0.5 cm thick, plain layer of compact mortar.

In front of the altar, the plaster layer US398 (6.0 cm in thickness and with no gravel) was laid down and completely surrounded pillars M418 and M421 (Fig. 17). Imprints in the plaster on the front part of the altar indicate that at this stage it was raised by a rectangular stone, in order to keep it separated from the facing area, thereby shaping it into a sort of basin with three higher sides.

Bench M415 later lost its function and was covered with plaster; to underline this change, a new shallow post hole was dug through its remains. This hole, US402, was meant to host the main post sustaining the roof after the removal of the earlier one in hole US395.[6]

[6] It is possible that a first replacement was attempted in the precise place of the old post, laying down a new base stone, which anyhow collapsed due to inaccurate filling of the underlying void.

FIGURE 16. *View from the north of the rectangular, plastered space standing in front of the altar in Phase VII. Delimited by benches, it embraced the two stone "pillars" M418 and M421.*

FIGURE 17. *A general view of the shrine in Phase VIII, from the west, showing the repeated plastering of floors, and how this had to face continuous ground movements due to the settling of the deposits laid down above Period 1's debris. The two decorated pillars S1494 and S1495 are not present since they were removed immediately after retrieval to prevent theft.*

Cultic/decorative elements possibly coming from more ancient phases of the shrine were dislocated near the altar. Apart from several incense burners, the most important finds are two limestone pillars decorated on one face with a high-relief image of a snake (S1494, S1495, Fig. 18 and cat. 17-18). This image is also important for identifying the dedicant of the shrine, likely unchanged through the different Periods (see below).

The last phase of Period 2 was characterized by a structural change that already indicates a severe decaying of the building (Plate 9). The eastern and northern walls were in fact capped with new rows of rough stones, named M247 and M249, causing a slight change of the overall plan of the shrine and making part of the benches no longer usable. Four new benches were placed directly on top of the earlier ones (anticlockwise from north, M405 to M408). No binder was used in their extremely poor construction.

Reconstruction of the walls' top, though inaccurate, apparently allowed the removal of the central post sustaining the roof,[7] and the new, equally poorly made bench M410 could be erected in the place of M415.

[7] Not that the possibility of an open air shrine can be ruled out.

FIGURE 18. *Detail of the two decorated pillars S1494 and S1495 placed against the altar's eastern side in Phase VIII, and englobed by later features. These pillars likely supported the incense burners retrieved in the collapse layer sealing the shrine US281.*

US387 was the floor associated to this phase, a compact layer of brown loam with an abundant quantity of mudbricks lumps, clearly laid down after the building of M410, from which a bronze hairpin (MB604) was collected.
Immediately before the substantial rearrangement of Period 3, a probable garbage pit was dug against the western flank of the altar and filled with bones, shells, a large amount of charcoal and one large iron slag (US287).

Period 3 (Phase X)

The final layout of the shrine is quite difficult to reconstruct due to collapses and late disturbances; nevertheless the room continued to be used within the frame of a residual occupation of the whole city (Plate 10). A substantial gap between the end of Period 2 and this new phase was witnessed by the remarkable raising of the entrance elevation, now at 29.73 m a.s.l.
While the northern bench was still in use, the altar zone underwent some minor changes, and an elevated earthen platform (US393) was built in front of the entrance. It covered bench M407 and was made up of compacted loam, framed at the top by a roughly set, sub-oval row of undressed stones.[8] A rectangular stone basin (S1203, cat. 5) was still sitting on the platform (Fig. 19). The

[8] Two other similar structures were discovered, one in the stores quarter (Area B) and the other inside the Monumental Building 1.

FIGURE 19. *General view of the shrine, Phase X, from the north. Note the rectangular basin S1203 standing on top of the sub-oval platform US393.*

connection with the lower parts of the room is not clear; the altar was probably reachable by walking down a couple of poorly made steps located east of the platform, but their layout must remain hypothetical due to bad preservation.

The final collapse

A massive accumulation of medium size stones and loose loam was the result of the shrine's definitive collapse. A series of artefacts were uncovered in this layer (US281) which strongly indicated the sacral function of the room from the very beginning of the excavation. But they also attested to a sudden and accidental end to the shrine's life. Apart from a series of more ordinary incense burners (S1207, S1208, S1209, S1218, cat. 13-16), including a shell possibly used for the same purpose (Sh359, cat. 49), a fragmentary limestone statuette of a lion (S1194, cat. 2) came to light, along with three decorated incense burners placed on truncated-conical bases, which stand out as high quality items (S1197, S1200, S1201; Fig. 20 and cat. 8-10). A fragment of an offering table (S1206, cat. 6), mortars (S1202, S1221, S1224, cat. 26-27, 29), a fragment of a stone mill/rotary quern (S1225, cat. 32) were discovered, along with a fragment of earring (MB526, cat. 39).

FIGURE 20. *The excavation of the massive, post-abandonment layer US281 led to the discovery of several relevant finds. Among these, various types of incense burners, like S1202 (a), S1200 (b), and S1201 (c).*

Radiocarbon dating of samples from this layer indicates a 2σ calibrated range between 54 and 288 AD (Fig. 30b). The thickness of US281 suggests that in this phase the higher parts of the shrine's wall could simply have been wattle and daub walls set on the remains of the more ancient stone walls.[9]

The cultural deposits linked with the shrine's life were finally sealed by US247, coming from the gradual decay of the walls mixed with aeolian accumulation. From US247 comes the limestone human head S1193 (cat. 1), probably meant to be set jutting out from a wall – so far the only example known in Oman.

[9] This is again consistent with the evidence gathered for other late period's buildings, of which only stone footings remains, often extremely ephemeral.

3. Some considerations on architecture and furnishing

The small shrine identified in room A110 and its original annex A152 is the second religious building excavated so far within the ancient city of Sumhuram, after the large temple discovered in Area F and dedicated to Sīn (Sedov 2008a). To these can be added an *extra muros* temple, excavated along the lagoon's coast to the west of the city (Pavan and Sedov 2008; Fig. 21). Chronologically, the urban shrine, with its structure possibly dating back to the most ancient monumental architectural layout of the city, would be earlier than its bigger counterpart in area F. The latter was in fact taken back to the second construction phase of the area, built above the ruins of an older building without any necessarily religious functions (Sedov 2008a: 187-190). No connections can be made with the stratigraphy of the *extra muros* temple, but it is noteworthy that the excavation of this small building bore a quantity of sherds that point to an early date (Sedov 2008c).

The urban shrine and the *extra muros* temple both have whitish plaster floors which in each case also cover the benches. This is quite unusual among the larger temples of Ḥaḍramawt, which are commonly paved with nicely worked stone slabs (Sedov 2005: 47), but is not surprising in the context of Sumhuram. In fact, several buildings of different typologies throughout the city show the same features, with completely plastered walls as well.[10] A furnace for the production of plaster was also excavated in the city, not far from the shrine.[11] This choice for the temples might point to a lack of stone material or on its excessive cost for the community; on the other hand, this simple kind of floor can be found in other small settlements' shrines in the Ḥaḍramawt as well, for example at Jujah and Bā Quṭfa (Hansen *et al.* 2004; Breton 1979).

The orientation along an east-west axis is the same as the Sīn temple in area F, but their entrances opened in opposite directions; although this could also depend on the need to adapt to the limited space inside the city, it nevertheless conforms to the norms for urban temples of the Ḥaḍramawt, usually oriented either along a north-south or an east-west axis, like the Shabwa temples or those in the Raybūn oasis.[12]

Almost all the features displayed by the shrine are common and widespread among Ḥaḍrami sacred buildings, and South Arabian ones more generally. Nevertheless it is hard to find any actual parallel in terms of layout and furniture.

---

[10] An example are the stores excavated in Area B in the late '90s (Morandi Bonacossi 2002: 39), and more recently during the campaign of May 2013 (=SUM13B), or the same rooms excavated immediately east of the shrine.

[11] The furnace has been excavated during the investigation of street A156 in the first campaign of 2011 (SUM11A). See the report at http://arabiantica.humnet.unipi.it/index.php?id=imto-khor-rori-sum11.

[12] See Sedov 2005a: 41-42. It is quite evident that the orientation of sacred buildings erected on wadis slopes conversely depended on the general morphology of the place.

FIGURE 21. *General view of the* extra muros *temple of Sumhuram (top), and a detail showing the building technique of its benches, made of rough stones and covered by the same plaster of the floor (bottom).*

The altar was clearly the main feature and focus of the shrine. Fitting parallels are scarce; a general idea of the original layout of the earlier, badly preserved altar M449 could be given by the one discovered in the Royal Palace of Shabwa (Fig. 22) and probably by a similar one (now demolished) in Timnaʿ.[13] On the basis of these examples, one can imagine a stepped structure with a C-shape polished stones frame, with two steps of almost the same width.

These parallels seem more convincing than the general similarities with the later altar M419 (Period 2) that lacks the stone "core" of the earlier. The tub-like appearance of the area in front of this later altar (including its late structure, which in a late phase was turned into a basin) recalls on the other hand a detail given in the description of the same Timnaʿ altar, on top of which a «plaster lined "tub"» (Darles 2009: 86-87) was reported.

Several plastered pits associated with the different phases of the shrine were brought to light, and were surely fundamental for the rites performed there. At least some of them could have been connected with the use of liquids during rituals. The importance of ablution before entering sacred places in South Arabian religion is well known. Moreover, liquids in general were constantly poured and offered on tables/altars comprised of gutters and runnels systems leading to basins sunk in the floor or draining liquids outside the temple.

This important role of water inside the shrine can be considered alongside the issue of the possible connection with the adjacent area. The hypothetical identification of the area immediately east of the shrine as a sort of "bath quarter"[14] (see the central rooms in Fig. 3), based on the widespread use of plaster covering both the floors and several walls of the unearthed premises, could in this respect find some support. Moreover, its proximity with the so-called Monumental Building 1, which hosts the only source of fresh water known so far inside the city, should also be added to this scenario. The "baths" could in fact satisfy the need for preventive ablution, and also provide the water needed for rituals, drawn from the adjacent Monumental Building 1. In Period 3, the wide basin retrieved served the same purpose, and perhaps it is no coincidence that at that same moment the old quarter had already been abandoned and was covered by thick deposits. Similar basins were retrieved also in the temple of Area F and in the *extra muros* temple, where they would also have been necessary in earlier phases, due to the distance from fresh water.

At the same time, some evidence would argue against this interpretation, and favor one that is also less peculiar within documented South Arabian buildings. The widespread use of plaster in different buildings of the city has already been mentioned; besides, a mortar housing for a rotary quern was retrieved in one of the premises of area A close to the shrine. Other specimens were found in more recent phases inside small rooms to the east of the shrine but still within the same area of the city, likely pointing to continuity in the function of area A. The layout of the structures connected with this rotary quern is far from clear, as they were rearranged several times and lay under more recent walls. Although the final study is not yet complete, it is possible

[13] Darles 2009: 86-87. It has anyhow to be underlined how these structures were not located in temples, and their interpretation as altar can somehow be disputable.

[14] Suggestion made by Prof. Christian Darles, that the authors would also like to thank for the useful discussions and the numerous advices given during his stay in Salalah. *Contra*, the opinion of Prof. Alexander V. Sedov, who, like the authors, considers the same structures linked with the processing of cereals (see below). It has to be stressed, anyhow, that the excavated layout of the area could be related to a late phase of occupation, and that it can not be excluded that it obliterated an earlier arrangement.

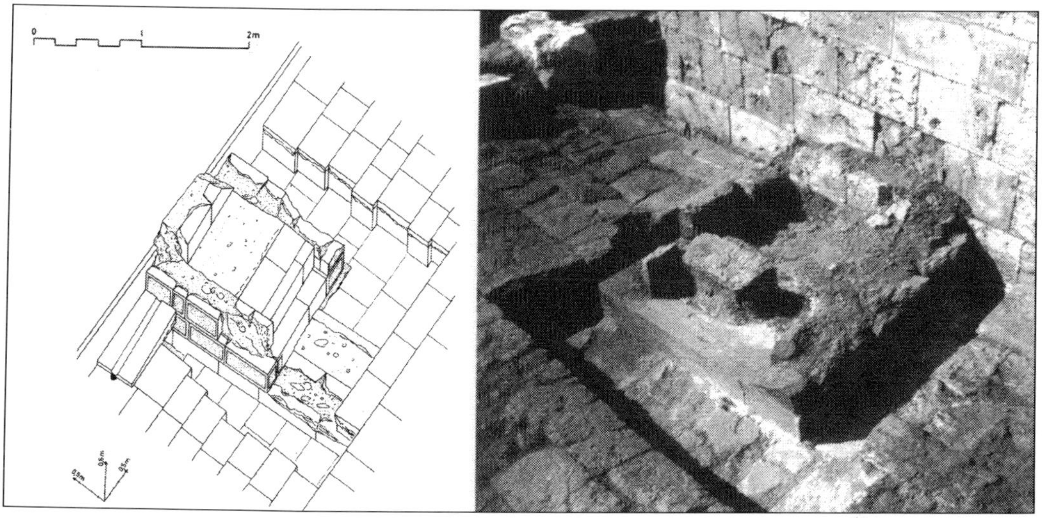

FIGURE 22. *Axonometric view and a picture of the altar in the Royal Palace of Shabwa (after Darles 2009: figs 9b and 8).*

to suggest that it probably belongs to an intermediate phase of this area's life, but likely later than the very first occupation of the city.[15] Regardless, one point is certainly clear: access to the premises located east of the shrine was only possible from the west, through a remarkably narrow, dogleg-shaped entrance located between the shrine and the Monumental Building 1. This likely indicates a strongly controlled activity with restricted access to the area. Such a situation is also evident in Monumental Building 1 itself, where its fresh water source was only accessible through a similar, dogleg shaped entrance. Similarly, activities in the storage quarter located in the southeastern part of the city were strictly controlled as only a small "sea gate" gave access to its central square. The proximity of the area to the shrine, in our specific case, might indicate a strong economic role for the religious structure, and the intriguing evidence for grain processing hints at the possibility that the temple owned agricultural land.

No offering table was found *in situ* in the shrine. The complete rectangular table found reused as a bench (S1538, cat. 7) could have had an earlier function in the shrine, but no evidence points to its placing.

Incense burners were certainly in use during Periods 2 and 3, but were probably already present in Period 1. The most remarkable of these are the three complete specimens found in US281 (S1197, S1200, S1201, cat. 8-10 – see below) and belonging to Sumhuram Type I, with composite shape on a truncated pyramidal base (Lombardi 2008: 317-325). They were found placed in front of the C-shaped altar M419. Two of them likely stood on top of the small prismatic elements with high relief snake (S1494, S1495, cat. 17-18) found set into the mortar near the eastern

[15] This is in particular made evident by the kind of quern, since rotatory querns are usually seen as deriving from a Roman influence, and thus not preceding the final decades of the 1st century BC.

side of the altar. A small amount of mortar was found still adhering to the top of these, as well as at the bottom of the burners. This placement could have lasted in Period 3 as well. Nothing definitive can be said for Period 1, but it is more than plausible that similar burners were placed close by the altar/podium M449, possibly exploiting the little niches on its sides. Cruder incense burners were found as well, and it is interesting to note the exclusive occurrence in the shrine of a set of roughly worked incense burners made from crumbly sandstone and roughly circular in shape (S1207-1209, S1218, cat. 13-16).

At least during one phase of Period 2, a removable bronze altar/footed offering table[16] was probably used, as indicated by bronze traces in the plaster in front of the altar.

Several of the stone and bronze tools and instruments discovered could be linked to ritual activities. Small size mortars (S1202, S1221, S1518, cat. 26-28) are consistent with the assemblage recovered in the temple of Sīn and in the *extra muros* temple and mostly belong to type III of the Sumhuram typology (Lombardi 2008: 330-333). A tall, truncated, cone-shaped mortar (S1507, cat. 30) as well as the fragmentary rotary quern S1225 (cat. 32) could be used for cereals. The red colour still visible on the edge of the rim of S1507, however, represents a treatment usually reserved for incense burners and supports its ritual value.

A small amount of pottery was found in the shrine, mainly in the later contexts whose chronological significance is discussed below. Finds were predominantly of storage vessels plus some cooking potsherds likely connected to the preparation of meals and/or ritual sacrifices or libations. Nor can the idea that ceramic vessels were also employed in fumigations be excluded. The scarce quantity of animal bones (completely absent in some of the layers), could indicate that the offerings mainly consisted of fruits, dates and cereals.

A few beads in different materials (stone, glass, shell, cat. 41-48) and a group of quartz dices (S1537, cat. 51), can also be considered offerings to the deities.

Even in the absence of any epigraphic document directly mentioning any gods, the temple, or votive offerings made there, all the evidence presented here is consistent with a sacred quality for the excavated building, and this continued for its entire existence.

Considering the shrine plan as a whole, there are a few details that deserve attention regarding the different arrangements of Period 1 and Period 2. In Period 1, the division of the main room into two halves finds no parallel among South Arabian documentation. Nevertheless, it gives to the shrine a typically South Arabian axial layout. In fact, if one takes into account only the southern half of the early shrine, the altar stands perfectly in front of the entrance, flanked by two structures (tanks or niches) for which a symmetrical layout can also be envisaged. Nothing can exclude that the symmetry was further enhanced by some sort of "movable" or perishable separation between this nave and the northern one (perhaps curtains or wooden structures standing on M447), but no evidence for it was collected.

In Period 2 the axiality is completely lost. Furthermore, the altar is no longer oriented toward the entrance and the space in front of it becomes gradually more "independent" from the western part of the room, giving the idea of a separation between the real *sancta sanctorum* of the temple and some sort of an *ante-cella*, although without a visible physical separation.

---

[16] Similar, for example, to the two altars conserved in the Louvre (Caubet and Gajda 2003: 1219-1242).

4. Ḥaḍrami influence and local adaptation: preliminary remarks on the small finds

It was shown above how different aspects of the urban shrine of Sumhuram show a general correspondence to South Arabian tradition. At the same time, small finds also show peculiar traits rather indicating the blending with a different tradition or taste, which could be tentatively correlated to a local elaboration by artisans working at the site. One must also consider the potential for taking inspiration, if not actual artefacts, from a Hellenistic *milieu*.

The repeated representation of the snake, appearing on pillars and columns throughout the different occupational phases of the shrine, is one of these striking aspects.

Traditionally considered as an amulet and sometimes linked to the god Wadd, the snake is rarely attested in evident connection with religious buildings, and the entwined serpents of the Banāt ʿĀd (Antonini 2004) are too geographically and chronologically distant to constitute a proper comparison. Considering the lack of such representations in Ḥaḍrami architectural decorations, it is possible to suggest that snakes at Sumhuram had a different meaning, deeply rooted in a local sub-stratum as attested by their continued presence.

From the destruction layers which mark the passage from the first to the second main Period came the bronze applique representing a lion (MB625, cat. 4), originally stuck in the wall's plaster. Cast in one piece, this artefact can be related to the Hellenistic tradition. In fact, the muzzle is depicted in the full-face, and its rather "fluid" and realistic composition is similar to the Timnaʿ lions[17] (Fig. 23) and to the decorative handle discovered in the temple of Sīn at Sumhuram[18] (Fig. 24). Conversely, it differs from the lion from Wādī Ḥarīb, which could be related with an "oriental" tradition (Arbach 2005: 21-33; ʿAlī ʿAqīl and Antonini 2007: 84-86, 232). A rather unusual detail of the lion is its tail twisted around its leg. A similar feature is visible on a stone relief from Ẓafār (Fig. 25). The radiocarbon date obtained for the same context of the applique (charcoal sample) indicated a chronological range from the late 2nd century BC to the early 1st century AD, thus fitting that of the Timnaʿ lions[19] and confirming their affiliation to the same cultural *milieu*.

Like the snake, the lion recurs in the decoration of Sumhuram's urban shrine. Besides a relief fragment representing an ungulate foot (S1519, cat. 23), a small full relief statuette was also found (S1194, cat. 2). This fragmentary rough figure totally lacks the fluidity of the applique. This fact, combined with its being made out of local limestone, could indicate that it was the work of a local craftsman.

---

[17] See ʿAlī ʿAqīl and Antonini 2007: 86-88, 233 also for the previous references.

[18] For the handle decoration in bronze (MB168) see Pavan 2008: 394, 396, pl. 32/4, pl. 59/4.

[19] The dating of the Qatabanian king Shahr Yagul Yuhargib, contemporary with the lions from Timnaʿ, is still debated. According to Avanzini it could be placed in the 2nd century BC (Avanzini 2008: 609-641); Antonini, *contra*, discussing South Arabian bronzes, placed the appliques between the 1st century BC/1st century AD (ʿAlī ʿAqīl and Antonini 2007: 233).

FIGURE 23. *The Timnaʿ lion riders Ja 120 (after Simpson 2002: 129, cat. 152-153).*

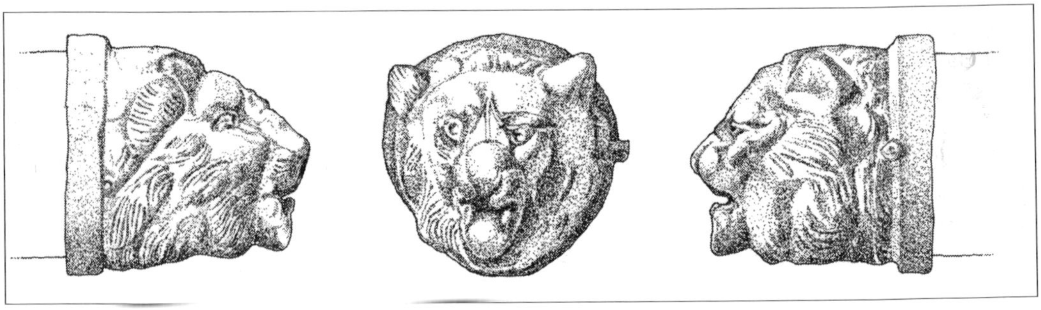

FIGURE 24. *Bronze handle MB168 from the temple of Sīn at Sumhuram (drawing by V. Labianca).*

FIGURE 25. *The relief from Ẓafār showing a lion with the tail twisted around its rear paw (Yule 2007: fig. 95).*

The hypothesis of a local manufacture can also be proposed for the limestone head found in the collapse layer which sealed the last occupational phase of the shrine (S1193, cat. 1). Carved in the same limestone employed for the city buildings, the back of the head features a protruding element meant to be inserted in a niche, as confirmed also by the inclination of the upper part of the head. The piece is quite unusual for both function and style: had it been unprovenanced, a link with a funerary context would have been the most plausible, but the discovery among the ruins of the shrine opens the way for different hypotheses: could it be the representation of a dedicant, or of a god? Also in this case the representation blends typical South Arabian traits (what remains of the hairdressing and the general geometrical layout of the representation) [20] with a local taste evident in the fleshy lips, in the protruding nose and in the circular and deeply carved eyes.

The same is true for the incense burners. The incense burner with lion and ibexes (S1197, cat. 8) is the most original among all the specimens discovered in Sumhuram, and finds no parallel in South Arabian documentation. It comprises a circular basin/reservoir standing on a parallelepiped-shaped element, surmounting a truncated-pyramidal base. Only the frontal side of the parallelepiped is decorated and shows a couple of ibexes flanking a lion on both sides. Ibexes, here depicted with great realism and attention to detail, are typical in South Arabian iconographic language, while the lion has a thick radiating mane which could represent a possible adoption and adaptation in stone of an original metal specimen. An identical radiated mane, in fact, characterizes the muzzle of a lion depicted on one of the short sides of a handled weight from Qaryat al-Fāw (Al-Ansary 1982: 88-89) and the same decoration adorns a bronze spout (MB339) discovered at Sumhuram (Fig. 26).

South Arabian tradition and regionalism also emerge in a second composite incense burner decorated with different images on its four sides (S1201, cat. 10): crescent and disk, a geometrical grid, an eagle, and a lion. While the first three motifs are rather typical – the eagle, for example, is represented standing facing right and with open wings on coins,[21] seals, and also on

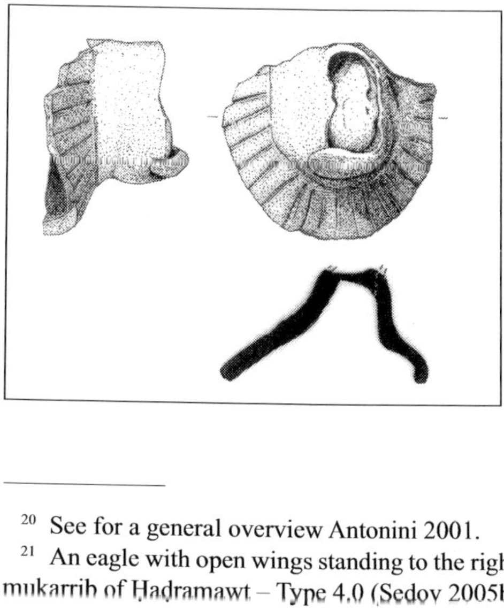

FIGURE 26. *Bronze spout MB339, from Sumhuram (drawing by S. Martelli).*

[20] See for a general overview Antonini 2001.

[21] An eagle with open wings standing to the right occurs in the reverse of the coinage of Yashhur'il Yuhar'ish, mukarrib of Ḥaḍramawt – Type 4.0 (Sedov 2005b).

figurate slabs although not in large number[22] – the lion's figure suggests a local craftsmanship, and further underlines the reverence for this animal. Interestingly, the base of the incense burner is decorated with projecting and recessing panels with vertical grooves placed exclusively on the protruding elements of the front side. Similar recessed panels occur on a tall incense burner from Sumhuram, M500, found during the American excavations and later published by Hassel (2002: 160, fig. 3).

The third complete incense burner (S1200, cat. 9) is, conversely, typically South Arabian. In its upper part geometrical elements (chessboard, false windows) occupy three faces with the fourth bearing the crescent and disk motif, while the base shows the same stepped decoration common to architectural elements like capitals and lintels of which S1533, reused as part of the Period 2 altar, is an example. This stepped base is occasionally found in connection with statuettes (Schmidt 2007: 208-209, pl. 13/2) but it is rarely attested for incense burners, for which it seems to be an archaic feature.

All these elements contribute to make of the shrine of Sumhuram an interesting example of religious architecture and templar furnishing that shows how "classical" South Arabian art was perceived and reinterpreted in a "provincial" centre.

[22] A slab representing an eagle with the same attitude has been discovered in Qāni', sector 1, Bâtiment B (Vinogradov 2010: 40, 64, fig. 23/283), but occurs also in a fragment at Museo Nazionale d'Arte Orientale "G. Tucci" in Rome (Pavan 2015: 70-71). In Ẓafar the eagle with open wings is a recurring motif on seals (see for example Yule *et al.* 2007: pl. 7/1a) and slabs and capitals (*ibidem*: pl. 22/3, pl. 25/1a).

5. Additional dating evidence from pottery, stone vessels and coins

A small amount of potsherds was discovered during the excavations of the shrine, mostly coming from the last occupational phases of the building. 92 fragments were collected: 80% belongs to storage vessels, 13% to table vessels and the remaining 7% to cooking vessels. The number of diagnostic pieces (rims, handles and bases) is limited to 12 potsherds (Fig. 27).
The most common type, albeit within this reduced sample, are jars standing on ring bases, made in a coarse and porous fabric and with a surface treatment limited to a wet smoothing. This is in line with the general trend observed at Sumhuram as a whole (Sedov and Benvenuti 2002: 182). These jars are commonly linked to Ḥaḍrami production due to the high number coming from the corresponding territory,[23] but they are actually known from the whole of South Arabia.[24]
In the same stratigraphic context a truncated-conical deep bowl was found, which shares with the mentioned jars the same coarse and porous fabric, pale yellow in colour.
Also worth noting is the presence of two fragments (belonging to the same vessel) of Black and Grey jar, a type of vessels most likely produced in the Gulf area. These jars can be connected with the storage of valuable goods (possibly dates), supported by the discovery of a similar potsherd in the *extra muros* temple (Sedov 2008c: 274-275, pl. 1/1).
The jars with coarse and porous fabric are dated to the final period of occupation of the shrine, about 3rd century AD, when this type of jar became predominant throughout the Ḥaḍramawt (Buffa 2015).
The Black and Grey jars can be tied to this same chronology, with their wider diffusion between the 2nd and the 3rd century AD (notwithstanding a rarer attestation from the 1st century AD).
The typology of storage vessels recovered in the shrine is completed by a fragment of a so-called hole-mouth jar, attributable to Period 2. This type is diagnostic for the Middle Period of Qāni' (Sedov 2007: 80, 89, fig. 4.16) and could be dated, according to the stratigraphic sequence of the shrine, to the 2nd century AD.
There were no significant finds from among the other potsherds except for the two fragments of cooking pots (Indian or in Indian style *handi*), discovered in Period 1 contexts and witnessing the importation of utilitarian vessels already during the early phases of the site's history.[25]

---

[23] See the occurrence of the type in Makaynūn (Benoist, Mouton and Schiettecatte 2005: 59-94), Jūja (Hansen *et al.* 2004: 43-67), Raybūn (Sedov 2003: 173-196, 245-291), Shabwa (Badre 1991: 303), Qāni' (Sedov 2010a: 209).

[24] Examples are known from the necropolis of Barāqish (Antonini and Agostini 2010: 35, 39), Timnaʿ (Buffa, personal communication), Hajar ibn Ḥumayd (Van Beek 1969: 115, 181), Ḥaṣī (Schiettecatte, personal communication), Jebel al-ʿAwd (Zech 2008).

[25] On the occurrence of imported utilitarian pots in the earliest period of occupation of the city, see Pavan and Schenk 2012.

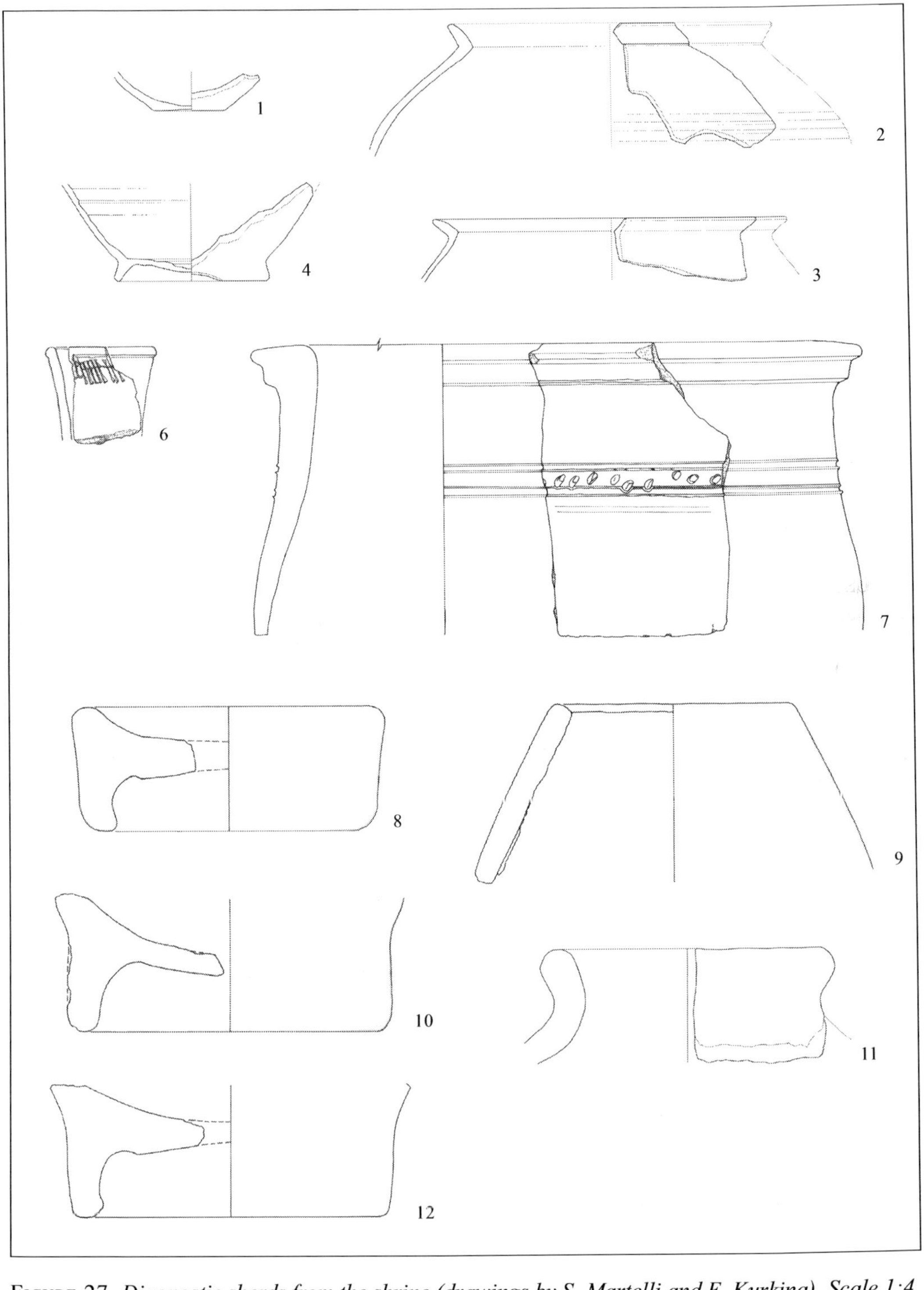

FIGURE 27. *Diagnostic sherds from the shrine (drawings by S. Martelli and E. Kurkina). Scale 1:4.*

POTTERY DESCRIPTIONS (FIG. 27)

US405 (Period 1, phase IV)

1. US405, 1: table jar, base, probably Indian; d. 4.0; th. 0.5; red compact fabric with white inclusions and mica; red section; external and internal surfaces: red (2.5YR4/6-10R5/6); slip and burnishing on the exterior.
2. US405, 2; globular cooking pot, fragment of rim; d. 20.0; th. 0.6; reddish compact fabric with white and dark inclusions and large amount of mica; external and internal surfaces: brown (7.5YR4/3); faint traces of slip on both surfaces.
3. US405, 3: cooking pot, fragment of rim; d. 22.0; th. 0.4; reddish compact fabric with white inclusions and mica; external and internal surfaces: dark red (10R3/6); slip on both sides; burnishing on the exterior; four horizontal parallel grooves below the rim on the exterior.
4. US405, 4: table jar, base and lower part of vessel; d. 10.0; th. 0.4; pinkish compact fabric with reddish inclusions and mica; external surface: brown (7.5YR4/4), internal surface: very pale brown (10YR8/3); slip on the exterior.

US392 (Period 2, phase VII)

5. US392, 1: hole-mouth storage jar, fragment of rim; d. 13.0; th. 0.7; reddish compact fabric with white lime grits and dark inclusions; dark grey core; external and internal surfaces: red (2.5YR5/6); wet smoothing on the exterior. (Not illustrated).

US388 (Period 2, phase VIII)

6. US388, 1: table jar, fragment of upper part; d. 6.8; th. 0.5; reddish compact fabric with dark and white inclusions, granite and large amount of mica; external and internal surfaces: dark grey (5YR4/1); slip on both sides; oblique lines deeply incised below the rim.

US 281 (Period 3, final collapse - phase X)

7. US281, 1+4: Black and Grey storage jar, fragment of upper part; d. 38.0; th. 4.1; reddish medium compact fabric with white and dark inclusions and mica; external surface: light brown (7.5YR6/3), internal surface: red (2.5YR4/6); thin wash; rice impressions decoration placed between two lines.
8. US281, 2: storage jar, high ring base possibly re-used as stand; d. 14.0; th. 2.0; coarse and porous fabric with white inclusions and straw temper; external and internal surfaces: reddish brown (5YR5/4); soot traces on the exterior; traces of plaster/gypsum in section.
9. US281, 3: storage hole-mouth jar, fragment of upper part; d. 13.0; th. 1.6; coarse fabric with reddish inclusions and straw temper; external and internal surfaces: pale yellow (2.5Y7/3); wet smoothing on the exterior.
10. US281, 5: storage jar, ring base; d. 22.0; th. 2,0; coarse and porous fabric with straw temper and white inclusions; external and internal surfaces reddish yellow (5YR5/6); thin wash on the exterior.
11. US281, 6: storage jar, fragment of upper part; d. 22.0; th. 2.1; coarse and porous fabric with straw temper and white inclusions; external surface: pale yellow (2.5Y7/4); internal surface: very pale brown (10YR7/4); wet smoothing on the exterior.
12. US281, 7: storage jar, fragment of ring base; d. 20.0; th. 2.1; coarse and porous fabric with straw temper and white inclusions; external and internal surface: red (2.5YR4/6); thin wash on the exterior.

Several fragments of soft-stone vessels were found during the excavations of the shrine. Most of them are, however, small, non-diagnostic wall pieces (S1214, S1215, S1216, S1227, S1232, S1487, S1491), which have been recorded but are not described nor illustrated.
For the other fragments (Fig. 28), when possible, reference is to Buffa's typology (Buffa 2008: 360-377).

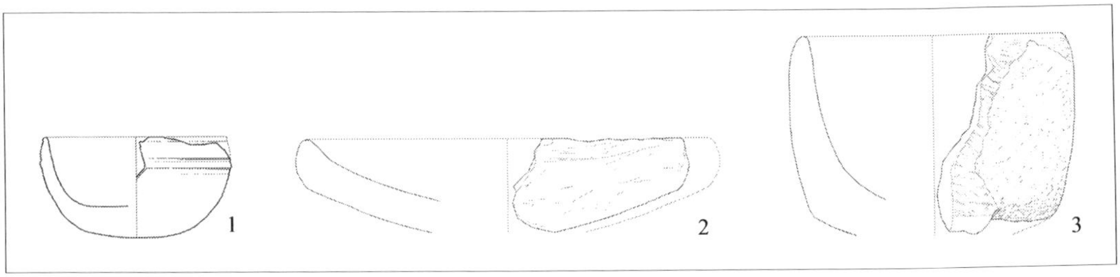

FIGURE 28. *Stone vessels' diagnostic fragments from the shrine (drawings by S. Martelli). Scale 1:3 (1); scale 1:6 (2-3).*

STONE VESSELS DESCRIPTIONS (FIG. 28)

1. S1530; US416, 6: Fragmentary small bowl; d. 7.0; th. 0.4 to 1.2.
   Wall thickening towards the base. Very highly polished outer surface, decorated by a slightly protruding line below the rim. Wheel marks on interior. For technique and material comparison see S464; S576 and S588 (Buffa 2008: 360, 353, 346, cat. 493, 378, 273). Fig. 28.1.
2. S1505; US405, 1: Fragment of pan; d. 30.0; th. 2.7.
   Short flared wall, flat base and rounded rim. Wide-bladed chisel marks on exterior, smoothed interior. Exterior slightly blackened by soot. Type I.1.c. Fig. 28.2.
3. S1508; US405, 3: Deep bowl; d. 19.0; th. 1.4.
   Convex profile and pointed rim. Exterior almost completely flaked, with traces of soot where the original surface is preserved. Well smoothed interior. Type II.4. Fig. 28.3.

Six coins were also discovered (Fig. 29).[26] All are in bronze and belong to Ḥaḍrami issues (Co643, Co628, Co630, Co472, Co475), with the exception of Co616, an excellent silver issue of remarkable quality which is easily identifiable as Ḥimyarite. The absence of wear traces on this coin suggests that it never actually circulated.
The chronological indications supplied by the coins generally fit in very well with the stratigraphy, confirming the sequence brought to light by the excavations (Table 1). Only the presence of coin Co475 – dated between the 4th and the early 2nd century BC – in a context of Period 3 has to be considered residual and does not compromise the proposed historical reconstruction.

[26] The information about the coins were kindly provided by Alexander Sedov.

FIGURE 29. *South Arabian coins found during the shrine's excavation. Scale 1:1, except no. 4: 1.5:1.*

COINS DESCRIPTIONS (A.V. SEDOV) (FIG. 29)

1. Co643; US417fl., 1; Period 1, phase I
Bronze; weight 2.1 g; 18x20 mm; die-axis on 12.00 o'clock; moulded, traces of cut mould-junctions on top and bottom.
Obv.: head r., big letter *m* (reversed) on l., legend on r. reads *[s]yn*; *rev.*: crude outline of eagle, legend on l. obliterated, legend on r. reads *[y]sh[h].*
Series *head/eagle*, Type 4.0, coinage of Yashhur'il Yuhar'ish, son of Abīyasa', *mukarrib* of Ḥaḍramawt (*circa* mid 2nd cent. BC) (Fig. 29.1).
2. Co628; US416, 2; Period 1, phase III
Bronze; weight 0.8 g; d. 14 mm; die-axis on 12.00 o'clock; moulded, traces of cut mould-junctions on top and bottom, unworked edges of flan.
Obv.: very faint traces of head r.; *rev.*: very faint traces of crude outline of eagle, legends obliterated.
Series *head/eagle*, Type 4.0, coinage of Yashhur'il Yuhar'ish, son of Abīyasa', *mukarrib* of Ḥaḍramawt (*circa* mid 2nd cent. BC) (Fig. 29.2).
3. Co630; US394, 7; Period 1, collapse of phase IV
Bronze; weight 5.8 g; d. 20; uncertain; regular flan with cracks around bevelled edges, slightly scyphate, broken.
Obv.: obliterated; *rev.*: traces of bull standing on line r., monogram on bottom r. obliterated, very faint traces of horizontal legend on top l., above the bull.
Series *radiated head/bull*, Type 5.3, coinage of Ilī'azz (?) (*circa* 1st cent. BC – mid 1st cent. AD) (Fig. 29.3).

4. Co616; US389, 1; Period 2, phase VII
Silver; weight 1.9 g; d. 13; die-axis on 10.00 o'clock; regular slightly scyphate flan (*very good quality without wear traces*).
Obv.: head r., linear border around interrupted on top r.; *rev.*: smaller on r., 'Yanaf' monogram on l., 'royal sign' on r., legend on top round from 2.00 o'clock reads *'mdn/byn*, legend in the exergue reads *rydn*.
Series *with two heads*, coinage of ʿAmdān Bayyin, king of Sabaʾ and dhū-Raydān (*circa* 80-100 AD). (Fig. 29.4).

5. Co472; US281, 10; Period 3, phase X
Bronze; weight 28.1 g.; d. 34.0 mm; very thick (5.0 mm) flan with bevelled edges, slightly scyphate, corroded and broken.
Obv. and *rev.* obliterated (Fig. 29.5).

6. Co475; US281, 18; Period 3, phase X
Bronze; weight 2.6 g; 7x10; die-axis uncertain; oval very thick (7.0 mm) flan.
Obv.: obliterated; *rev.*: very faint traces of owl.
Series *head/owl*, Type 1.1 or 1.2 (legend is not determined), Anonymous coinage (*circa* mid 4th – early 2nd century BC) (Fig. 29.6).

Co643	US471fl.	*head/eagle* – type 4.0	*circa* mid 2nd century BC
Co628	US416	*head/eagle* – type 4.0	*circa* mid 2nd century BC
Co630	US394	*radiated head/bull* – type 5.3	*circa* 1st cent. BC – mid 1st cent. AD
Co616	US389	*with two heads*	*circa* 80-100 AD
Co472	US281	not id.	not id.
Co475	US281	*head/owl* – type 1.1/1.2	*circa* mid 4th cent. – early 2nd cent. BC

TABLE 1. *Chronology of the shrine's coins, arranged following the stratigraphic sequence.*

6. Conclusive remarks on the shrine's chronology

Both the outline of three main construction phases for Sumhuram and the surrounding territory recently proposed by Alexander Sedov,[27] as well as the recent consideration of the chronology of Alessandra Avanzini (2014), finds a clear confirmation in the stratigraphy of the shrine, where three occupational periods were distinguished, as described in the previous pages.
Although the small finds are of little help in dating the different periods and phases due to the lack of peculiar or distinctive features, the coins and the ^{14}C dates can be used to fit the architectural changes into an absolute chronological frame.

Period 1 (phases I-IV)
The first period is characterized by a sequence of three different floors (from the most ancient: US417, US416 and US406), the latest covered by a number of layers (US405, US394) which are to be linked with an (accidental?) destructive episode, followed by a deliberate deposition of loam and debris. While US405 is connected with the probable collapse of the second floor or roof of the building (see above), US394 can be interpreted as the preparation layer for the foundation of a new floor (US391) corresponding to the first phase of Period 2.
Co643, discovered on US417floor, identified as an issue of Yashhur'il Yuharʿish, son of Abīyasaʿ, *mukarrib* of Ḥaḍramawt, is to be considered a good marker to fix the chronology of the construction of the shrine to the 1st century BC as well as Co628, belonging to the same issue, coherent with the 2σ calibrated date (106 BC-71 AD) obtained from a charcoal sample collected in US405 (Fig. 30a).
Further consistency to this sequence is given by Co630, found in the thick layer US394. The coin belongs to the series *radiated head/bull* (Type 5.3), issued by Ilīʿadh, who ruled around the mid 1st century AD.
Hence, the initial foundation of the shrine can be likely dated around the end of the 1st century BC, while the end of Period 1 has to be placed in the early/middle 1st century AD.

Period 2 (phase V-IX)
Period 2 is defined in the shrine by the sequence of floors US391, US390, US389, US388 and US387. The only dating element recovered from contexts belonging to this period is a Ḥimyarite

27 The chronology of the site has been recently discussed by A.V. Sedov, during the 17th edition of the Rencontres Sabéennes held in Paris between the 6th and the 8th of June 2013. The authors wish to thank Alexander Sedov who kindly provided the text of his communication.

coin (Co616 from US389) issued by ʿAmdān Bayyin, king of Saba' and dhū-Raydān (circa 80-100 AD). Only two silver specimens of the series with two heads were collected at Sumhuram (Co616 and Co511),[28] and the coin coming from the shrine is even more peculiar by virtue of its perfect state of conservation. This could speculatively be seen as an indication that it never circulated, and suggests that it was part of some kind of offering or templar "treasure". Be that as it may, the date associated with the kingdom of ʿAmdān Bayyin can be attributed to US389floor, and is consistent with the final date defined for Period 1. The chronological frame for Period 2 thus spans from the early/middle 1st century to, tentatively, the first quarter of the 3rd century AD (see below).

Given such a chronological setting it is worth noting that the "re-foundation" of the shrine, corresponding to Period 2, can probably be listed among the numerous architectural interventions carried out in the city under the Ḥaḍrami king Ilīʿadh, the same mentioned in the inscription KR2 as the promoter of construction works in the city "from the base to the top" (Avanzini 2002: 130; more recently, Avanzini 2008: 634-636). To this king we can attribute the re-arrangement of the city gate, as well as the second main constructional phase of the so-called Monumental Building 1 – with the general and imposing raising of its walls (Pavan and Degli Esposti in preparation) –, in addition to many other renovation works throughout the city.

Period 3 (phase X)

The last period of occupation is poorly represented, a consequence of heavy collapse and later disturbances. Nevertheless, the function of the room is clear despite a completely different arrangement. Particularly notable is the erection of an earthen platform (US393) near the entrance. The remains of this last occupational phase were buried under the final collapse of the shrine, US281, from which numerous small finds of high quality and interesting manufacture were collected. This confirmed, on the one hand, the importance and the function of the building also in this later phase and, on the other, the sudden and probably accidental end of the shrine.

The 2σ calibrated range obtained from a charcoal sample collected in US281 reveal a chronological span between 54 and 228 AD (Fig. 30b). The latter date fits in very well with our chronological reconstruction, which places the end of Period 2 around the early 3rd century AD. Period 3 represents the late phase of wealth of the shrine (and of the city), suddenly compromised by an unknown event which buried all the noteworthy items inside the temple under a massive collapse (US247) which decisively sealed the cultural deposit.

After this event only ephemeral occupation took place nearby the shrine's ruins, the only faint traces of which are the scanty remains of poorly made dwellings. No hint of a chronological definition of this phase is available, and its continuation until the 5th century AD is merely a hypothesis based on the general chronology of the site.

[28] For Co511 see the database on-line: imtodb.humnet.unipi.it.

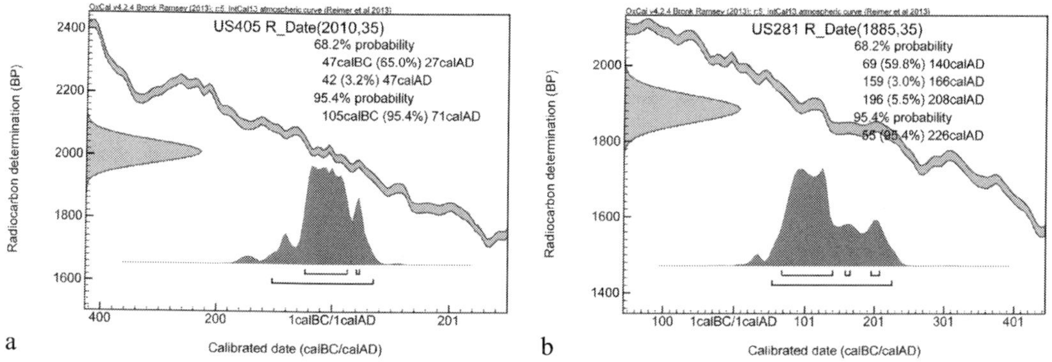

FIGURE 30. *Radiocarbon dates for contexts US405 and US281. Calibrated with OxCal v. 4.2.4, IntCal13 atmospheric curve (Bronk Ramsey 2013; Reimer et al. 2013).*

ACKNOWLEDGEMENTS

The authors would like to thank Prof. Alessandra Avanzini (University of Pisa, Dipartimento di Civiltà e Forme del Sapere) for the opportunity to take part in the excavation of the shrine and for supporting the publication of this work inside the series "Quaderni di Arabia Antica".

Silvia Lischi, former student at Pisa and now also a member of the Italian Mission To Oman is acknowledged for the help provided on the excavation as she supervised part of the work while the authors were not on the field.

Prof. A. Sedov was so kind to read a preliminary version of the text, making corrections and giving invaluable advices. Evan M. Rap has to be thanked for editing an earlier version of the English text (Chapters 1-6). Interpretations and any remaining error are solely the responsibility of the authors.

Alessandra Lombardi is gratefully acknowledged for the precious work of editing and page layout, and for constant advising on these issues.

Bronze objects from Sumhuram discussed and illustrated in the text were restored by Gianluca Buonomini.

Works of the Italian Mission To Oman are strongly supported by the Office of His Excellency the Adviser to His Majesty the Sultan for Cultural Affairs – Muscat and Salalah (Sultanate of Oman).

Further information on the IMTO activities and preliminary reports for all the seasons of excavation conducted at the site can be found at http://arabiantica. humnet.unipi.it.

7. Catalogue of small finds

by Alexia Pavan

The measures of the objects are in cm:
height = h.; widht = w.; thickness = th.; diameter = d.; depth = dp.

Stone and Bronze Statuary

1 – Stone head
S1193; US247, 1 pls 13/1; 23/1
Limestone; h. 16.0; w. 15.0; th. 16.0
Period 3; final collapse of the shrine
Complete human head, flaked on the upper right corner. The shape is roughly squared with deeply incised circular eyes (d. 1.7), rounded eye-brows, bar nose – fragmentary on the lower part – and mouth with slightly protruding inferior lip. The forehead is short, the chin quite flat with rounded edges; ears are missing. Every detail suggesting the gender of the represented figure is lacking. On the back there is a projecting element (17.0x6.8x5.0) to fit the object into a cave space, probably inside a niche or in a wall. The surface is roughly smoothed and the quality of the stone rather poor. The crude style of execution could suggest a local manufacture.

2 – Lion statuette
S1194; US281, 1 pls 13/2; 23/3
Limestone; l. 24.5; w. 8.2; h. 9.6
Period 3; Phase X
Fragmentary and poorly preserved animal statuette depicting a lion. One of the hind legs is partially preserved, but the three others are totally missing except for where they connect with the body, where the stone has been carved and incised to show the muscles and the hair. The snout is rather poorly preserved, but open jaws showing three canines are recognizable, as well as the mane which frames only the upper part of the muzzle. A small, circular depression indicates the presence of the right eye. Roughly smoothed surface.

3 – Stone snake
S1529; US405, 11 pls 13/3; 23/2
Limestone; l. 11.3; w. 4.0; th. 2.6
Period 1; end of Phase IV
Object in shape of snake. Head and part of the body are preserved. A number of circular cavities were carved to represent the animal's skin. The head is rhomboidal in shape with two holes placed on both sides representing the animal's eyes.

4 – Bronze lion applique
MB625; US405, 12 fig. 9; pl. 14
Bronze; h. 8.0; w. 10.0; th. 0.4
Period 1; end of Phase IV

Complete bronze applique depicting a lion. The animal is represented in profile but with frontal head. The four legs, arranged to suggest movement, stand above a trapezoidal base with a thin protruding step. The mouth is open, suggesting an aggressive attitude, with canine teeth clearly visible. The upper tail is missing, while the lower tail is twisted around the leg.

Templar Furnishing

5 – Basin
S1203; US281, 8 pl. 24/1
Limestone; l. 73.5; w. 51.0; h. 31.2
Period 3; Phase X
Complete stone basin with rectangular shape, roughly worked on the exterior where chisel marks are evident. The interior has been smoothed by water.

6 – Offering table
S1206; US281, 9 pl. 24/2
Limestone; l. 22.2; w. 16.2; th. 9.0
Period 3; Phase X
Fragment of corner of offering table with raised flat frame (w. 4.8; dp. 0.7). All sides are carefully smoothed except for the base where there is evidence of chisel marks. Signs of secondary burning are visible on the top surface and on the frame.

7 – Offering table
S1538; M443, 1 pl. 24/3
Sandstone; l. 87.0; w. 29.0; th. 15.0
Period 1; Phase III
Rectangular offering table, broken in two parts. One end with plain gutter is preserved (measures of the gutter: 14.0x6.0x2.0). There is a recess (2.5 deep on the top), with frame (5.0 wide), raising up all along the margins. Chisel marks are visible along the edges. The offering table has been re-employed, turned upside down, as part of bench M443.

Incense Burners

8 – Incense burner
S1197; US281, 2 pls 15; 25/1
Limestone; l. max 23.0; w. max. 19.0; h. max. 33.0
Period 3; Phase X
Complete incense burner standing on a truncated-pyramidal base (15.0x20.0x18.0), irregular in plan. The upper part is made of a rectangular element (23.0x18.5x10.5) surmounted by a circular cup (d. 16.8; th. 1.8; dp. 2.8). The top of the rectangular element has been roughly carved in the shape of two small, irregular, triangles.
The most interesting feature is the decoration of the main face which consists of three animals: a lion in the centre and two ibexes at the sides. The lion is frontal with the forelegs terminating in claws worked in

full relief and standing on a short protruding support (measures of the support: 2.5x5.5x0.7). The lion has a thick radiating mane which frames the lower part of the muzzle and covers the upper part of the legs. The tufts of fur are realized with small incisions around the muzzle. On the lion's forehead rests a kind of headgear resembling a horned tiara which is completely uncommon in the South Arabian iconography. The muzzle is characterized by incised almond eyes and carved circular pupils. The lion has open jaws with the canines preserved. On its sides there are two ibexes represented in profile with the muzzle turned towards the interior. Other features include tongue barbs, circular carved eyes, small pointed ears, ribbed horns and small pointed tails. The composition is not perfectly symmetrical as the right hand ibex has its hind legs and back slightly raised. Behind the ibex there is also an unclear element, possibly representing a couple of arrows.

Traces of burning are visible inside the cup. With the exception of the front decorated panel, execution is rather rough. The limestone used for the object is of rather poor quality. Such material compares closely to the masonry blocks used in the city, and so the object could be considered a product of a local manufacture.

9 – Incense burner

S1200; US281, 5 pls 16; 25/2

Limestone; l. 14.5; w. 13.0; h. 31; dp. 2.4

Period 3; Phase X

Tall incense burner, complete except for three elements at the corners of the cubic element placed on its top. The base is made of three trapezoidal steps projecting outwards. It stands on a rectangular basement (measures: 14.0x11.5x2.5) and recalls the support for statuettes sometimes found in South Arabian temples (Schmidt 2007: 208-239, pl. 13/2) or the bases of some incense burners from the Jawf (Arbach and Audouin 2007: 39, n. 21; Arbach and Schiettecatte 2006: 54-55, pl. 13/39,59, pl. 14/43). Oblique chisel marks are visible on all the elements at the base. At the top sits a cubic censer measuring 13.5x15.2x12.0. A rectangular element projecting upward from one corner (likely the only preserved one out of four identical elements) measures 4.0x3.7x4.5. Two of the faces are decorated with a chessboard motif made of four rows of squares of variable dimensions (from 3.7x1.8 to 2.2x1.7) realized in low and high relief. Such a pattern recalls the crosshatching pattern common to South Arabian burners. The same motif is visible also on plaster coating in Al-ʿUqla (Darles 1998: 168, fig. 6). The third face is decorated with alternating projecting and recessed rectangular panels of varying sizes (projecting panels: 3.0x10.8; recessing ones: 2.0x10.8). The fourth face, likely the front, presents the typical South Arabian astral motif of the crescent moon with a disk inside (d. 3.5), representing the Sun or Venus, standing on a trapezoidal element. No burning traces or blackened surfaces were noticed. As already suggested by Alessandra Lombardi (2008: 319) it is probable that a small container could have been placed inside the censer.

10 – Incense burner

S1201; US281, 6 pls 17; 25/3

Limestone; h. max. 31.0; dp. 2.2

Period 3; Phase X

Tall incense burner with high truncated pyramid-shaped base (h. 18.0; bottom 12.8x12.7; top 11.5x12.2) and cubic censer at the top (15.5x15.5x13.0). It is decorated with four standing elements at the corners (4.5x4.5x1.5).

On three of the four sides the base is decorated with alternating projecting and recessed panels (average width: 3.6). Vertical grooves are visible only on the protruding elements of the front. Similar recessed panels also appear in a tall incense burner found in Sumhuram during the American excavations and later

published by Hassel (2002: 160, fig. 3). The fourth side, identified as the back, is plain. The four faces of the censer are decorated with different scenes or motifs.
On the front is the astral motif of the crescent moon with the disk inside (Sun or Venus) placed on a trapezoidal base. The surface is quite worn and the representation not clearly readable.
The lateral faces present respectively an eagle with opened wings and hook-beak and a lion or panther with raised tail. The eagle, represented also on some Ḥaḍrami coins (Type 4.0, head/eagle series), seldom occurs on stelae or figurative slabs (see discussion in Chapter 4). The feline has slim body with thin legs ending with large claws. On the head is a rounded eye and a muzzle with sticking out tongue and two canines visible. The back side of the censer has a chessboard decoration with squares slightly incised on the surface (2.1-2.3x1.5-1.7). Chisel marks are clearly visible on the back. Inside the censer there is a deep squared cavity with traces of burnt substances. The object is poorly worked and the surfaces are not carefully smoothed, especially on the base.

11 – Incense burner
S1503: US394, 1 pl. 26/1
Limestone; l. 9.8; w. 9.8; h. 8.5
Period 1; collapse of Phase IV
Fragment of a squat, squared incense burner, poorly preserved. The flat base originally sat on squared legs – three preserved – (measures: 3.1x3.3x1.6), placed at the corners. The rim, with trapezoidal cross section, is almost completely missing. The internal recess is roughly carved. Traces of burning and chisel marks are visible inside and on the top. The lateral faces are straight without any decoration.

12 – Incense burner
S1504; US394, 2 pl. 26/2
Limestone; l. 12.0; w. 10.0; h. 8.8
Period 1; collapse of Phase IV
Small fragment of limestone object, badly preserved, probably an incense burner. The scanty remains seem to suggest a truncated cone-shaped base with an upper element, probably rectangular.

13 – Incense burner
S1207; US281, 11 pl. 26/3a
Sandstone; h. 5.0; d. max. 11.0
Period 3; Phase X
Irregularly circular and roughly carved incense burner with flat base. The sides are carelessly made, with evident chisel marks visible also on the top of the object, concave in shape (dp. 1.5). Along with the similar pieces S1208, S1209 and S1218, S 1207 belongs to a new type of incense burners, previously unattested in Sumhuram and occurring exclusively in the shrine. The function of this object is confirmed by blackening on the top and by the material from which it was made: a soft, crumbly sandstone unsuitable for utilitarian items.

14 – Incense burner
S1208; US281, 12 pls 18/1; 26/3c
Sandstone; h. 5.0; d. max. 12.0
Period 3; Phase X
Sub-triangular incense burner with flat base, roughly carved. Concave top with visible chisel marks (dp. 1.3), irregular in shape.

15 – Incense burner
S1209; US281, 13 pl. 26/3b
Sandstone; h. 6.7; d. max. 13.0
Period 3; Phase X
Irregularly circular, roughly carved, incense burner with flat base. The sides are carelessly made with visible chisel marks.

16 – Incense burner
S1218; US281, 23 pl. 26/3d
Sandstone; l. 19.0; w. 14; h. 6.5; d. 7.0
Period 3; Phase X
Fragmentary object identified as an incense burner because of the similarity with S1207, S1208 and S1209. No burning traces are evident in the object, but the crumbly material is not appropriate for crushing or grinding, supporting its interpretation as incense burner.

Architectural Elements

17 – Pillar
S1494; US398, 1 pls 18/2; 27/1
Limestone; h. 37.0; w. 15.0; th. 13.0
Period 2; Phase IX
Pillar comprising a three-stepped squared base (15x13x10.5) and a truncated-pyramidal vertical element (13x11.5x26.5), with the representation of a snake on the front. The top of the pillar is not preserved but it was probably flat and used to host a different object, possibly an incense burner. There are clear traces of a fresh break, caused by an attempt of theft while the pillar was in situ. The pillar is decorated with a representation of snake in bas-relief with wavy body and pointed tail. The head, probably rhomboidal in shape, is missing along with the top of the object.

18 – Pillar
S1495; US398, 2 pls 18/3; 27/2
Limestone; h. 41.0; w. 17.0; th. 13.0
Period 2; Phase IX
Fragmentary pillar with composite shape, decorated with a snake on the front. The back is recessed to allow it to fit into a different space. The top and the bottom are both missing. The snake is represented in bas-relief with wavy body, pointed tail and rhomboidal head. A circular protuberance on the left side of the head could represent one of the eyes. Traces of plaster are visible near the base. The limestone employed for the pillar is of rather poor quality.

19 – Pillar
S1539; M443, 2 pl. 18/4
Limestone; h. 25.0; w. 13.0; th. 10.0
Period 1; Phase III
Fragmentary pillar, rectangular in shape and section, bearing the representation of a snake in low-relief on the main face. All the faces of the pillar were intentionally smoothed, with the back less carefully carved.

Since the head and tail of the animal are lacking, it is likely that the pillar was re-worked on the shorter sides, probably during its reuse. According to comparisons with similar pieces we can hypothesize the presence of a rhomboidal head and a pointed tail.

20 – Decorated block
S1531; M419, 1 pls 19/1; 27/3 right
Limestone; l. 41.0; w. 19.0; h. 22.5
Period 2; Phase V
Architectural element, rectangular in shape and section, decorated on one of the small faces. All the sides are smoothed. The top has a raised frame (th. 1.2-1.7) and two rectangular cavities (one almost completely missing), the other measuring 2x3.1x0.3. Their function seems connected to the placement of the object. The most interesting feature is the decoration of the front, where is depicted a crescent moon atop a trapezoidal base with a disk inside it. On the top and on the lateral sides is a framework made from a series of dentils alternating with the plain surface in a very low relief. Two rows, placed horizontally, are clearly visible on the top of the representation; the rows placed vertically at the sides are quite eroded. The object was found during the dismantling of the altar M419. Like S1532, it has been re-employed. The original position is not identifiable.

21 – Decorated block pls 19/2; 27/3 left
S1532; US416, 7
Limestone; l. 42.0; w. 20.0; h. 24.5
Period 2; Phase III
Architectural element, rectangular in shape and section, decorated on one of the small faces. All sides are smoothed. The top has a raised margin (th. 1.2-1.7) and two rectangular cavities, one almost completely missed (3x3x1.6; 2x3x1.5). The cavities, as in S1531, are both placed 14 cm from the corner. Their function seems to be connected to the fixing of the object (cavity for clamps?). There are no visible traces of bronze inside, however. The main representation stands inside a framework made of squares alternating plain surface in very low relief. Above the horizontal row of squares, it is possible to distinguish the representation of merlons, probably depicting the façade of the temple. In the lower part there is the representation of the moon crescent with the solar disk inside. It's not possible to hypothesize the original position.

22 – Lintel
S1533; US390, 2 pl. 28/1
Limestone; l. 96.0; w. 23.0; h. 17.0
Period 2; Phase VI
Architectural element, identified as a lintel, rectangular in shape and composite in section. The frontal face is decorated with a three-stepped geometrical motif. The steps have different height: two measure 5.0 and one – presumably the lowest – 4.5. The section comprises two recesses, located in correspondence to the back corners. One measures 2.0x4.0, the other 5.0x4.5. They were employed to fix the lintel in place. The lintel was found re-employed, but the most probable original location is the entrance to the shrine.

23 – High relief fragment
S1519; US405, 5 pl. 20/1; 28/2
Bronze; l. 6.7; w. 2.0; h. 3.5
Period 1; collapse of Phase IV

Fragmentary object, comprising a base and an upper part depicting the paw of an animal, presumably a lion, according to the shape of the toe nails. The base seems to be finished on the bottom, so the fragment could be interpreted as lion statuette standing on a rectangular base.

24 – Decorated block
S1514; US394, 3 pl. 28/3
Sandstone; l. 6.8; w. 5.8; h. 5.8
Period 1; collapse of Phase IV
Fragment of object, missing of one of the lateral sides. The most interesting feature is the decoration of the main face which depicts the motif of a false window. It is placed near the corner and it seems to run the full height of the object. The window is carved in low relief, underlined by a framework and decorated with horizontal lines. The colour of the objects (grey) suggest possible burning (fire inside A110?). For comparisons see TC1235 and TC1240 (Cleveland 1965: 139, pl. 95).

25 – Architectural element
S1540; US394, 10 pl. 28/4
Limestone; l. 33.0; w. 6.5; h. 10.5
Period 1; collapse of the first shrine
Architectural element broken at both extremities. It was found re-employed in the plaster tank near wall M449. The object is rectangular in shape and section and is decorated on one of the main faces with a thin groove, placed 3.0 cm below the top, which runs horizontally across the whole surface. It is not possible to identify the original function or position, although it surely served as an architectural decoration.

Stone Tools

26 – Mortar
S1202; US281, 7 pls 20/2; 29/1
Dark granite; h. 10.0; d. base 20.3; d. rim 15.5
Period 3; Phase X
Although it is not a clearly identifiable artefact, this object was classified as a mortar because of its shape and its section. It lacks any traces of grinding or pounding operations. The object is complete, except for a breakage along the rim and on the top of the wall. The base is slightly rounded on the margins. The rim is well defined, with concave face (dp. 2.7). Of particular note is the high quality of the polishing technique, which rendered the upper surface completely smoothed. Considering the traces of combustion visible at the time of discovery, it is possible the object was reused as a censer. The object could also be interpreted as a ritual tool employed exclusively for particular substances. The special function of the object is further supported by the material, a dark granite usually not employed in Sumhuram for the mortars, except for S163.

27 – Mortar
S1221; US281, 26 pls 20/3; 29/2
Limestone; h. 11.0; d. max. 19.5; dp. max. 2.5
Period 3; Phase X
Complete mortar with irregularly convex base and walls, not carefully smoothed. It also has an irregularly

concave top surface with a maximum depth of 2.5. The rim is not precisely defined, but determined by the limits of the upper surface and progressive concavity. The burning traces on the top suggest a secondary use as burner.

28 – Mortar
S1518; US394, 4 pl. 29/3
Stone; h. 5.8; d. 14.6
Period 1; Phase IV
Complete small, rounded mortar, with flat base. The external wall is slightly convex; the rim rounded and internal cavity concave. Presence of a semicircular protuberance along the rim (l. 2.7, th. max. 1.9). The protruding semicircular element could be compared with the hemispherical "ear-lug" in the bowls of type IX from Ḥureiḍha (Caton Thompson 1944: 123, pls. XXXII/1-8; LIV/10-11, 13-14).

29 – Mortar
S1224; US281, 29 pl. 29/4
Stone; h. 5.5; d. 24.0
Period 3; Phase X
Fragment of mortar, preserved for one quarter. The base is flat and slightly rounded on the sides. The slightly rounded rim is quite eroded. Smoothed surface. For comparison see S580, S603.

30 – Mortar
S1507; US405, 2 pls 20/4; 29/5
Limestone; h. 27.0; d. max. 25.0; th. 3.6
Period 1; Phase IV
Fragment of tall, truncated cone-shaped mortar, slightly squared on two sides. The internal cavity is 19.0 deep. The surface is roughly worked and not refined by smoothing; chisel marks are clearly visible on both the internal and external wall. The top of the rim is flat and painted in red, a treatment usually reserved for incense burners.

31 – Mortar
S1522; US405, 10 pl. 20/5
Limestone; h. 6.5; d. 10.5
Period 1; Phase IV
Complete small, rounded mortar, with flat base, rounded at its margins. The external wall is slightly convex; the rim is rounded. The internal, circular cavity is concave (dp. 1.6). The surface is flaked. The object appears to have been burnt during a strong fire.

32 – Millstone
S1225; US281, 30
Stone; h. 5.0; d. 28.0
Period 3; Phase X
Fragment of circular object, identified as the lower stone of a rotary quern, less than a quarter preserved. The base is flat and slightly rounded on the top and on the bottom; the external wall is straight. In its centre is a clearly defined cavity (dp. 3.5; d. not recognizable) probably to fix the wooden stick around which the quern rotated.

Instrumenta

33 – Handle
MB626; US394, 6 pl. 30/1
Bronze; l. 6.9; d. 3.0; th. 0.1
Period 1; collapse of the first shrine
Circular bronze handle with four rivet holes.

34 – Handle
B67; US431, 1 pl. 30/2
Animal bone; l. 2.5; d. 0.7
Period 1; Phase II
Fragment of handle, cylindrical in shape, with smoothed surface.

35 – Nail
MI159; US405, 4 pl. 30/3
Iron; h. 3.0; d. max. 2.2
Period 1; collapse of the first shrine
Iron nail with circular section stem and rounded flat head. The tip is missing.

36 – Nail
MI160; US405, 9 pl. 30/4
Iron; h. 4.8; d. max. 0.9
Period 1; collapse of the first shrine
Fragment of iron rod or nail; only one end is preserved.

37 – Plaque
MB605; US396, 1 (room A152) pl. 30/5
Bronze
Period 1; Phase IV
Thin bronze plaque made from fragments of different size. The shape was probably rectangular. In the corners there are four holes, probably for fixing to another surface. The surface is corroded.

Personal adornments

38 – Pin
MB604; US387, 2 pl. 21/1
Bronze; l. 8.0; d. 0.4
Period 3; Phase X
Pin lacking the tip, circular in section and with flattened end.

39 – Earring
MB526; US393 ,1 pl. 21/2
Bronze; l. 1.2; d. 0.3

Period 3; Phase X
Fragment of earring.

40 – Earring
MB528; US281, 19 pl. 21/3
Bronze; l. 1.4; d. 0.3
Period 3; Phase X
Fragment of earring.

41 – Bead
S1509; US416, 1 pls 21/4; 31/1a
Orange carnelian; h. 0.5; d. 0.4
Period 1; Phase III
Bead with circular shape, flattened ends, irregular in section. Well polished surface.

42 – Bead
S1526, US416, 3 pl. 21/5; 31/1b
Pisolite (sedimentary rock); h. 0.6; d. 0.7
Period: 1; Phase: III
Spheroid bead with flattened ends and slightly eccentric hole. Polished surface with some chippings.

43 – Bead
G142, US416, 4
Glass; h. 0.6; d. 0.5
Period: 1; Phase: III
Small bead with flattened ends. D. hole 0.2. Very smoothed surface.

44 – Bead
Sh358, US416, 5 pl. 21/6; 31/1c
Conus shell; h. 0.8; d. 1.5
Period 1; Phase III
Irregularly rounded and convex bead, made from the apical part of a *Conus* shell. Slightly eccentric hole (d. 0.4). Irregular margins and height

45 – Bead
G140, US405, 7 pl. 21/7; 31/1d
Glass; h. 0.6; d. 0.7
Period 1; Phase IV
Spheroid bead with irregular hole. Slightly exfoliated surface. A small blue vein is visible near the hole. The conical hole perforating the bead seems to indicate a furnace-wound manufacture.

46 – Bead
G141, US405, 8 pl. 21/8; 31/1e
Glass; h. 0.6; d. 0.7
Period 1; Phase IV

Oblate bead with central hole (d. 0.1). The surface is not well preserved and it appears quite flaked. Whitish colour with blue veins.

47 – Bead
S1535, US394, 8 pl. 21/9; 31/1f
Pisolite (sedimentary rock); h. 0.7; d. 0.7
Period 1; collapse of Phase IV
Spheroid bead with slightly eccentric hole. Polished surface with some chippings.

48 – Bead
S1501, US405, 13 pl. 21/10; 31/1g
Carnelian; h. 0.8; d. 0.95
Period 2; Phase VII
Truncated, biconical bead with circular cross-section. The hole has been bored from one end and it is slightly eccentric. Polished surface with some chippings along the surface.

Varia

49 – Oil lamp
Sh359; M443, 3 pl. 31/2
Chlamys Townsendi shell; h. 16.5; l. 16.0
Period 1; Phase III
Complete oil lamp or incense burner, made from a *Chlamys Townsendi* shell, with scant burning traces inside.

50 – Pierced stone
S1196; US247, 2 pl. 22
Sandstone; h. 33.5; w. 23.0; th. 8.0
Period 3; final collapse of the shrine
Complete rectangular slab with flat section. One of the sides is decorated with three vertical incised lines covering the entire length of the surface of the slab. On the top, 2.0 cm below the edge, is a circular hole passing through the entire object (d. 1.3).

51 – Dices
S1537; US394, 9 pl. 31/3
Quartzite
Fifty-one rounded small, flat stones. The material has been identified as quartzite. They were found in three different layers (US394, US405, US416), but concentrated all in the same area of the shrine. Their unusual concentration suggests that they were used probably as dice or game pieces.

Bibliography

ʿAlī ʿAqīl A. and Antonini S. 2007. *Bronzi sudarabici di periodo pre-Islamico*. Paris: de Boccard; Rome: IsIAO.

Al Ansary A.R. 1981. *Qaryat al Faw. A portrait of pre-Islamic civilization in South Arabia.* Riyadh: Riyadh University Press.

Antonini A. 2001. *La statuaria sudarabica in pietra.* (Repertorio iconografico sudarabico, 1). Paris: de Boccard; Rome: IsIAO.

Antonini A. 2004. *I motivi figurativi delle Banāt* ʿĀd *nei templi sudarabici.* (Repertorio iconografico sudarabico, 2). Paris: de Boccard; Rome: Herder.

Antonini A. 2008. Due leoni/appliques da Nashshan (Jawf, Repubblica dello Yemen), *Egitto e Vicino Oriente* 31: 213-218.

Antonini S. and Agostini A. 2010. *A Minean necropolis at Barāqish (Jawf, Republic of Yemen). Preliminary Report of the 2005-2006 archaeological campaigns.* With an appendix by Paola Pagano. (Report and Memoirs. New series, 9). Rome: IsIAO.

Arbach M. and Audouin R. 2007. *Ṣanʿāʾ National Museum. Part II. Collection of epigraphic and archaeological artifacts from al-Jawf sites.* Ṣanʿāʾ: UNESCO-SFD.

Arbach M. 2005. Un lion en bronze avec un nouveau synchronisme minéo-qatabānite, pages 21-29 in A. Sholan, S. Antonini and M. Arbach (eds), *Sabaean Studies. Archaeological, epigraphical and historical studies in honour of Yūsuf M. ʿAbdallāh, Alessandro de Maigret, Christian J. Robin on the occasion of their sixtieth birthdays.* Naples: Università degli studi di Napoli l'Orientale.

Arbach M. and Schiettecatte J. 2006. *Catalogue des pièces archéologiques et épigraphiques du Jawf au Musée National de Ṣanʿāʾ.* Ṣanʿāʾ: Centre français d'archéologie et de sciences sociales de Ṣanʿāʾ.

Avanzini A. 2008. Notes for a history of Sumhuram and a new inscription of Yashhurʾil, pages 609-641 in A. Avanzini (ed.), *A port in Arabia between Rome and the Indian Ocean (3rd C. BC-5th C. AD). Khor Rori Report 2.* (Arabia Antica, 5). Rome: «L'Erma» di Bretschneider.

Avanzini A. 2014. Un port d'Arabie entre Rome et l'Inde, *Comptes Rendus de l'Académie des Inscriptions et Belles Lettres*: 483-505.

Avanzini A. (ed.) 2002. *Khor Rori Report 1.* (Arabia Antica, 1). Pisa: Edizioni Plus.

Avanzini A. (ed.) 2008. *A port in Arabia between Rome and the Indian Ocean (3rd C. BC-5th C. AD). Khor Rori Report 2.* (Arabia Antica, 5). Rome: «L'Erma» di Bretschneider.

Avanzini A. and Sedov A.V. 2005. The stratigraphy of Sumhuram: new evidence, *Proceedings of the Seminar for Arabian Studies* 35: 11-17.

Badre L. 1991. Le sondage stratigraphique de Shabwa 1976-1981, *Syria* 68: 229-314.

Benoist A., Mouton M. and Schiettecatte J. 2005. Makaynūn, un centre régional antique dans le Ḥaḍramawt oriental, pages 59-94 in A.M. Sholan, S. Antonini and M. Arbach (eds), *Sabean Studies. Archaeological, epigraphical and historical studies in honour of Yūsuf M. ʿAbdallāh, Alessandro de Maigret and Christian J. Robin on the occasion of their sixtieth birthdays*. Naples: Università degli studi di Napoli l'Orientale.

Breton J.-F. 1979. Le temple de Syn ḏ-Ḥlṣm à Bâ-Quṭfah (République démocratique et populaire du Yémen), *Raydān* 2: 185-202.

Bronk Ramsey C. and Lee S. 2013. Recent and planned developments of the program OxCal, *Radiocarbon* 55/2-3: 720-730.

Buffa V. 2008. Soft-stone vessels, pages 360-377 in Lombardi A., Buffa V. and Pavan A., Small finds, pages 317-475 in A. Avanzini (ed.), *A port in Arabia between Rome and the Indian Ocean (3rd C. BC-5th C. AD). Khor Rori Report 2* (Arabia Antica, 5). Rome: «L'Erma» di Bretschneider.

Buffa V. 2015. Shape Versus Ware. The South Arabian Straw Tempered Ovoid Storage Jars. 3rd Cent BC – 5th Cent AD, *Archäologische Berichte aus dem Yemen* 14: 47-61.

Buffa V. and Sedov A.V. 2008. The residential quarter: Area A, pages 15-59 in A. Avanzini (ed.), *A port in Arabia between Rome and the Indian Ocean (3rd C. BC-5th C. AD). Khor Rori Report 2.* (Arabia Antica, 5). Rome: «L'Erma» di Bretschneider.

Caton Thompson G. 1944. *The Tombs and Moon temple of Hureidha (Hadhramaut).* (Reports of the Research Committee of the Society of Antiquaries of London, 13). Oxford.

Caubet A. and Gajda I. 2003. Deux autels en bronze provenant de l'Arabie Méridionale, *Comptes rendus des séances de l'Académie des Inscriptions et Belle Lettres*: 1219-1242.

Cleveland R.L. 1965. *An ancient South Arabian necropolis. Objects from the second campaign (1951) in the Timnaʿ cemetery.* (Publications of the American Foundation for the Study of Man IV). Baltimore: Johns Hopkins Press.

Darles Ch. 1998. Le sanctuaire d'Al-ʿUqla, pages 163-169 in J.-F. Breton (ed.), *Fouilles de Shabwa III. Architecture et techniques de construction.* (Bibliothèque archéologique et historique, 154). Beirut: Institut Français d'Archéologie du Proche Orient.

Darles Ch. 2009. Des formes et des formules architecturales originales?, pages 83-107 in J.-F. Breton (ed.), *Fouilles de Shabwa IV. Shabwa et son contexte architectural et artistique du 1er siècle avant J.-C. au IVe siècle après J.-C.* Ṣanʿāʾ: CEFAS; Damas-Beirut-Amman: IFPO.

Hansen D.P., Ochsenschlager E.L. and Al-Radi S. 2004. Excavations at Jujah, Shibam, Wadi Ḥadramawt, *Arabian Archaeology and Epigraphy* 15: 43-67.

Hassel J. 2002. Cuboid incense-burning altars from South Arabia in the collection of the American Foundation for the Study of Man: some unpublished aspects, *Arabian Archaeology and Epigraphy* 13: 157-192.

Lombardi A. 2008. Stone objects, pages 317-360 in Lombardi A., Buffa V. and Pavan A., Small finds, pages 317-475 in A. Avanzini (ed.), *A port in Arabia between Rome and the Indian Ocean (3rd C. BC-5th C. AD). Khor Rori Report 2.* (Arabia Antica, 5). Rome: «L'Erma» di Bretschneider.

Morandi Bonacossi D. 2002. Excavation at Khor Rori, the 1997 and 1998 campaigns, pages 29-52, in A. Avanzini (ed.), *Khor Rori Report 1.* (Arabia Antica, 1). Pisa: Edizioni Plus.

Morandi Bonacossi D. 2004. Coloni hadramiti e popolamento indigeno nel paese dell'incenso (Dhofar, Sultanato dell'Oman) fra V sec. A.C. e VI sec. D.C. Una sintesi preliminare, pages 179-216 in F.M. Fales and D. Morandi Bonacossi (eds), *Mesopotamia e Arabia. Scavi archeologici e studi territoriali delle Università Trivenete (1994-1998).* Venice: Istituto veneto di scienze, lettere ed arti.

Pavan A. 2008. Metal objects, pages 377-397 in Lombardi A., Buffa V. and Pavan A., Small finds, pages pages 317-475 in A. Avanzini (ed.), *A port in Arabia between Rome and the Indian Ocean (3rd C. BC-5th C. AD). Khor Rori Report 2.* (Arabia Antica, 5). Rome: «L'Erma» di Bretschneider.

Pavan A. 2015. Symbolism and realism: the representation of animals, pages 66-71, in AA.VV., *Insights into ancient South Arabia. The collection of the Museo Nazionale d'Arte Orientale "G. Tucci" in Rome.* Pisa: Dedalo.

Pavan A. and Schenk H. 2012. Crossing the Indian Ocean before the Periplus: pottery assemblages in comparison. The sites of Sumhuram (Oman) and Tissamaharama (Sri Lanka), *Arabian Archaeology and Epigraphy* 23: 191-202.

Pavan A. and Sedov A.V. 2008 Religious Architecture in Sumhuram: the *extra muros* temple, pages 261-272 in A. Avanzini (ed.), *A port in Arabia between Rome and the Indian Ocean (3rd C. BC-5th C. AD). Khor Rori Report 2.* (Arabia Antica, 5). Rome: «L'Erma» di Bretschneider.

Pavan A. and Degli Esposti M. *in preparation*. Water and power. Excavations inside the so-called Monumental Building 1 at Sumhuram.

Reimer P.J., Bard E., Bayliss A. *et al.* 2013. IntCal13 and Marine13 Radiocarbon Age Calibration Curves 0-50,000 Years cal BP, *Radiocarbon* 55/4: 1869-1887.

Schmidt J. 2007. Das Heiligtum des Almaqah in Sirwah. Vorläufiger Bericht über die ersten beiden Grabungskampagnen 1992-1993, *Archäologische Berichte aus dem Yemen* 11: 208-239.

Sedov A.V. 2003. Notes on the stratigraphy and pottery sequence at Raybūn I settlement (Western wādī Ḥaḍramawt), *Arabia* 1: 173-196; 245-291.

Sedov A.V. 2005a. *Temples of ancient Ḥaḍramawt.* (Arabia Antica, 3). Pisa: Edizioni Plus.

Sedov A.V. 2005b. Ḥaḍramawt coinage: its sequence and chronology, *Archäologische Berichte aus dem Yemen* 10: 161-172.

Sedov A.V. 2007. The port of Qana' and the incense trade, pages 71-111 in D.P.S. Peacock and D. Williams (eds), *Food for the Gods. New light on the Ancient Incense Trade.* Oxford: Oxbow.

Sedov A.V. 2008. Area A: Pottery, pages 61-123 in A. Avanzini (ed.), *A port in Arabia between Rome and the Indian Ocean (3rd C. BC-5th C. AD). Khor Rori Report 2.* (Arabia Antica, 5). Rome: «L'Erma» di Bretschneider.

Sedov A.V. 2008a. The cultual quarter: Area F, pages 183-213 in A. Avanzini (ed.), *A port in Arabia between Rome and the Indian Ocean (3rd C. BC-5th C. AD). Khor Rori Report 2.* (Arabia Antica, 5). Rome: «L'Erma» di Bretschneider.

Sedov A.V. 2008b. Area F: Pottery, pages 216-259 in A. Avanzini (ed.), *A port in Arabia between Rome and the Indian Ocean (3rd C. BC-5th C. AD). Khor Rori Report 2* (Arabia Antica, 5). Rome: «L'Erma» di Bretschneider.

Sedov A.V. 2008c. *Extra muros* temple: Pottery, pages 274-275 in A. Avanzini (ed.), *A port in Arabia between Rome and the Indian Ocean (3rd C. BC-5th C. AD). Khor Rori Report 2.* (Arabia Antica, 5). Rome: «L'Erma» di Bretschneider.

Sedov A.V. 2010. Les fouilles du secteur 3, pages 87-122 in J.-F. Salles and A.V. Sedov (eds), *Qāni'. Le port antique du Ḥaḍramawt entre la Méditerranée, l'Afrique et l'Inde. Fouilles russes 1972, 1985-1989, 1991, 1993-1994.* (Indicopleustoi, Archaeologies of the Indian Ocean 6). Turnhout: Brepols.

Sedov A.V. 2010a. Les fouilles du secteur 6, pages 183-281 in J.-F. Salles and A.V. Sedov (eds), *Qāni'. Le port antique du Ḥaḍramawt entre la Méditerranée, l'Afrique et l'Inde. Fouilles russes 1972, 1985-1989, 1991, 1993-1994* (Indicopleustoi, Archaeologies of the Indian Ocean 6). Turnhout: Brepols.

Sedov A.V. 2010b. Les fouilles de la nécropole, pages 283-286 in J.-F. Salles and A.V. Sedov (eds), *Qāni'. Le port antique du Ḥaḍramawt entre la Méditerranée, l'Afrique et l'Inde. Fouilles russes 1972, 1985-1989, 1991, 1993-1994.* (Indicopleustoi, Archaeologies of the Indian Ocean 6). Turnhout: Brepols.

Sedov A.V. and Benvenuti C. 2002. The pottery of Sumhuram: general typology, pages 177-248 in A. Avanzini (ed.), *Khor Rori Report 1.* (Arabia Antica, 1). Pisa: Edizioni Plus.

Simpson St. J. (ed.) 2002. *Queen of Sheba. Treasures from ancient Yemen.* London: British Museum Press.

Van Beek G. 1969. *Hajar bin Ḥumeid: investigations at a pre-Islamic site in South Arabia.* (Publications of the American Foundation for the Study of Man, 5). Baltimore: Johns Hopkins Press.

Vinogradov, Yu. A. 2010. Les fouilles dans la partie sud-ouest du site. Le secteur 1, pages 11-64 in J.-F. Salles and A.V. Sedov (eds), *Qāni'. Le port antique du Ḥaḍramawt entre la Méditerranée, l'Afrique et l'Inde. Fouilles russes 1972, 1985-1989, 1991, 1993-1994* (Indicopleustoi, Archaeologies of the Indian Ocean). Turnhout: Brepols.

Yule P. 2007. *Himyar. Spätantike im Jemen/Late antique Yemen.* Aichwald: Linden soft.

Yule P., Franke K., Meyer C., Nebe G.W., Robin Ch. and Witzel C. 2007. Ẓafār, Capital of Ḥimyar, Ibb province, Yemen, Preliminary Reports 1-4, Summer 1998 until Spring 2004, *Archäologische Berichte aus dem Yemen* 11: 479-546.

Zech J. 2008. *Die Keramik der befestigen Höhensiedlung das Jabal al-'Awd im nordjemenitisches Hochland frühhimyarischer Zeit.* Unpublished dissertation, Freie Universität, Berlin.

Plates

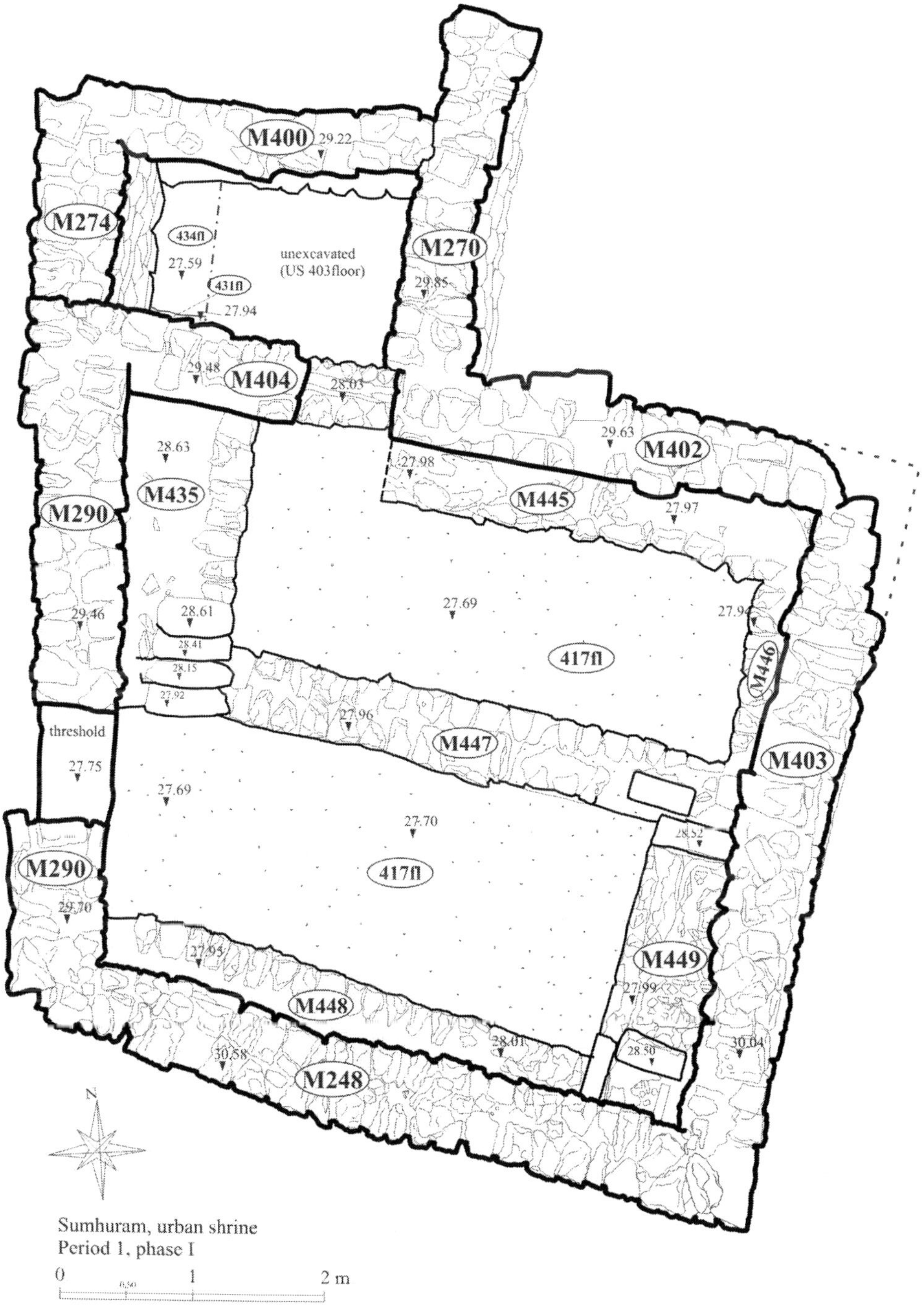

Plan of the shrine: Period 1, Phase I. Room A152 in use, north of main room A110.

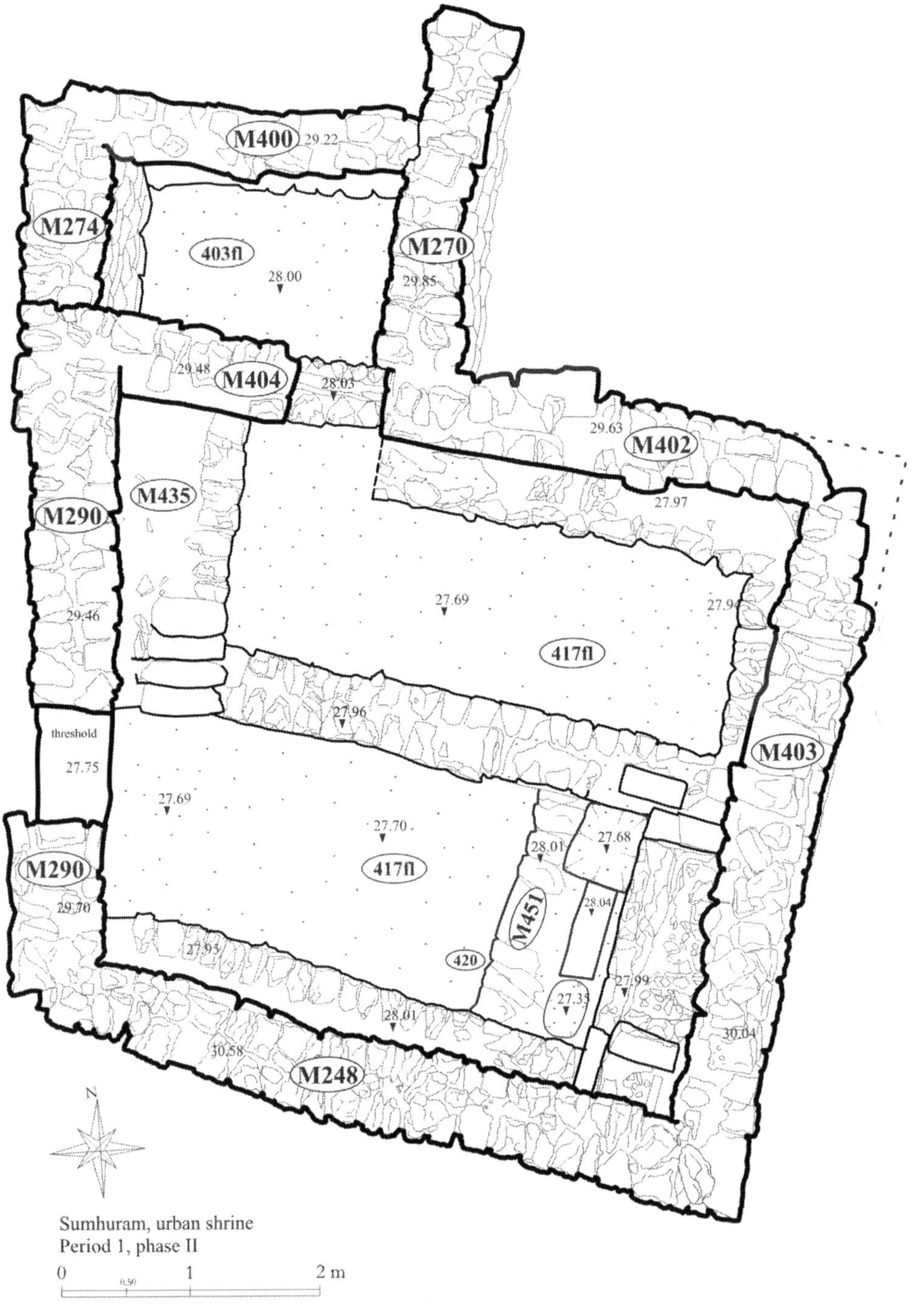

Plan of the shrine: Period 1, Phase II.

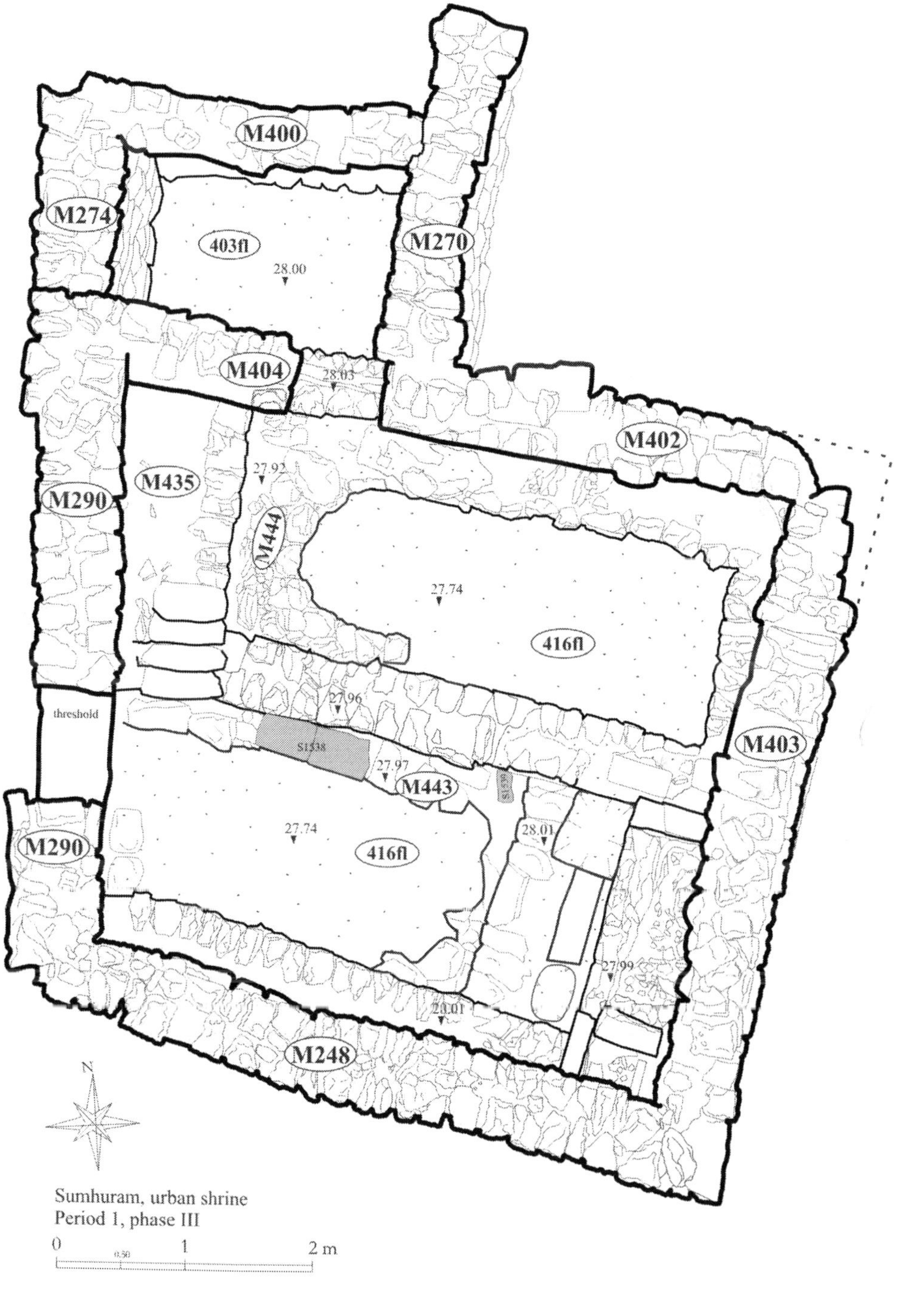

Plan of the shrine: Period 1, Phase III.

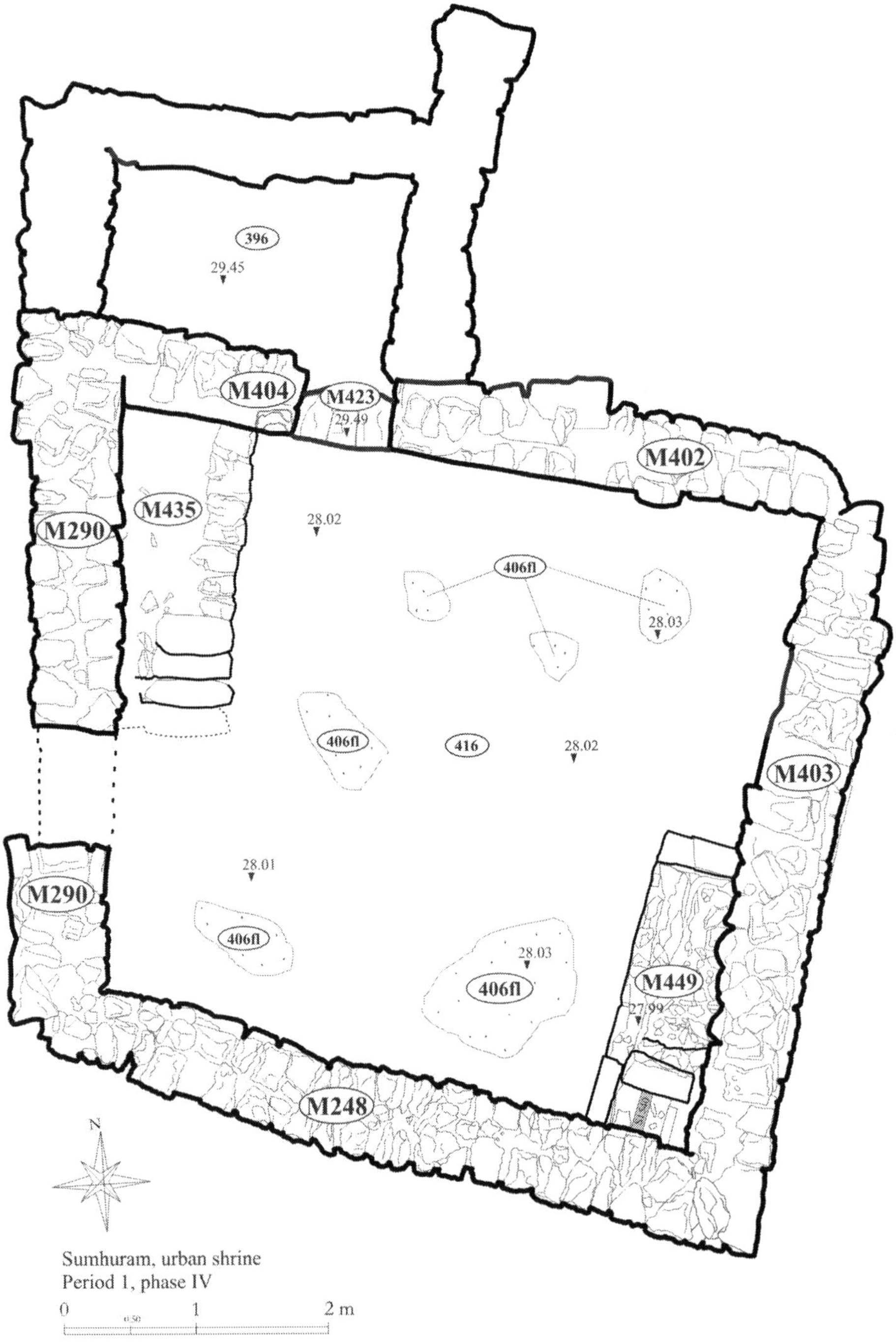

Plan of the shrine: Period 1, Phase IV.

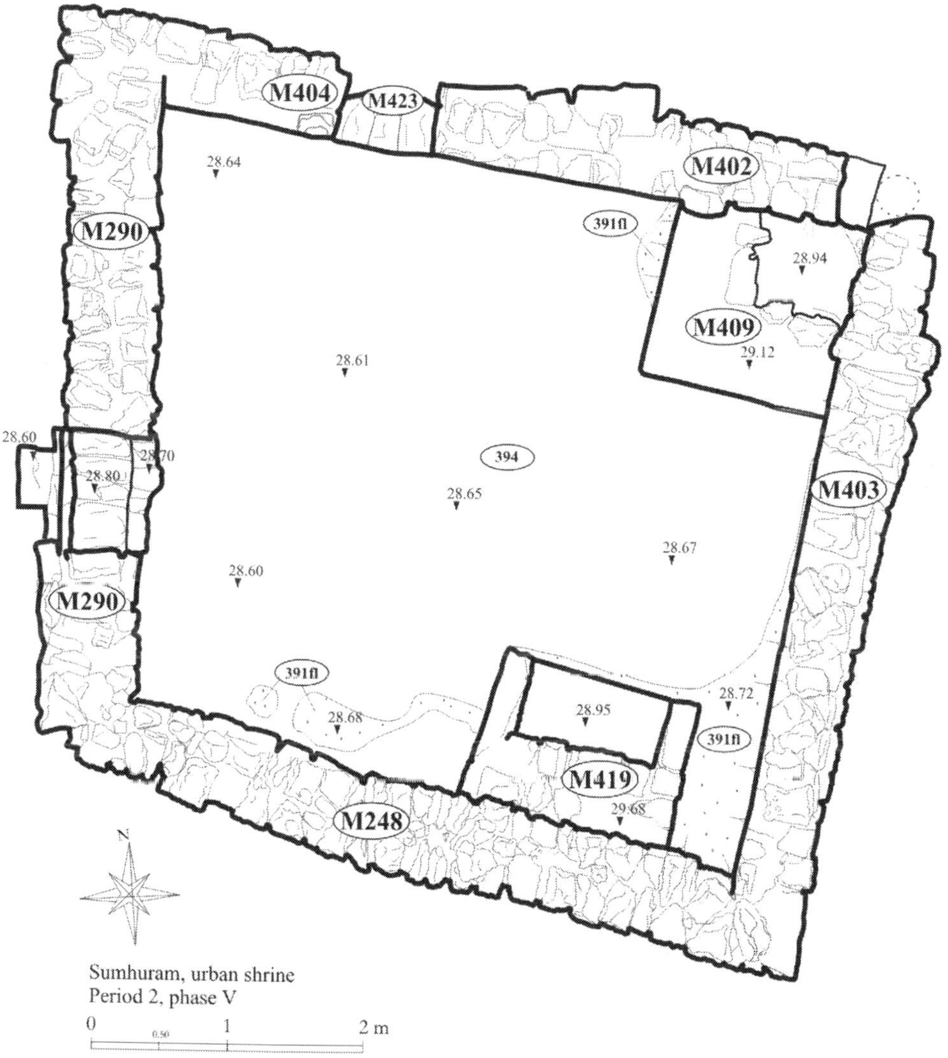

Plan of the shrine: Period 2, Phase V. Room A110 no longer in use.

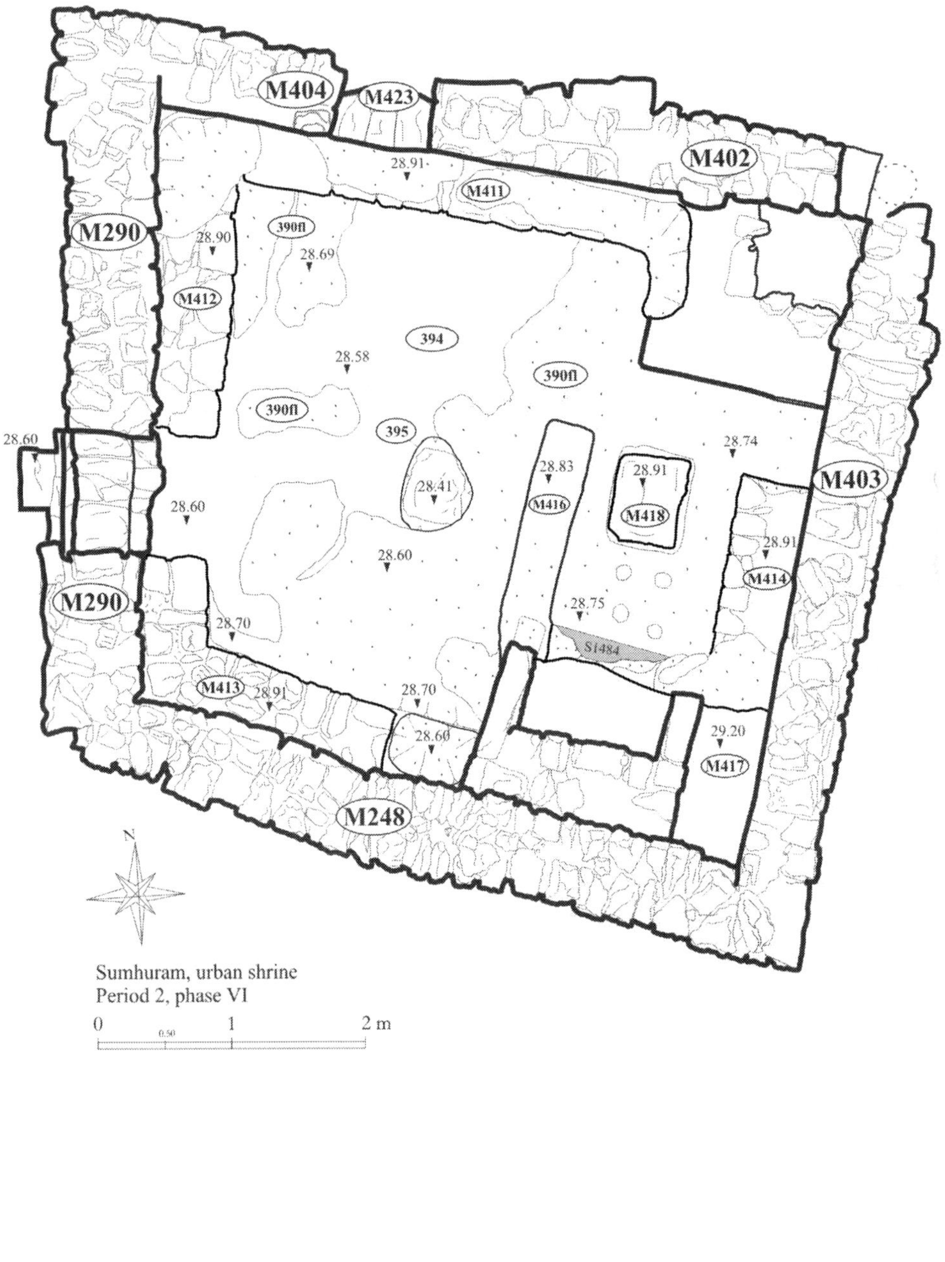

Plan of the shrine: Period 2, Phase VI.

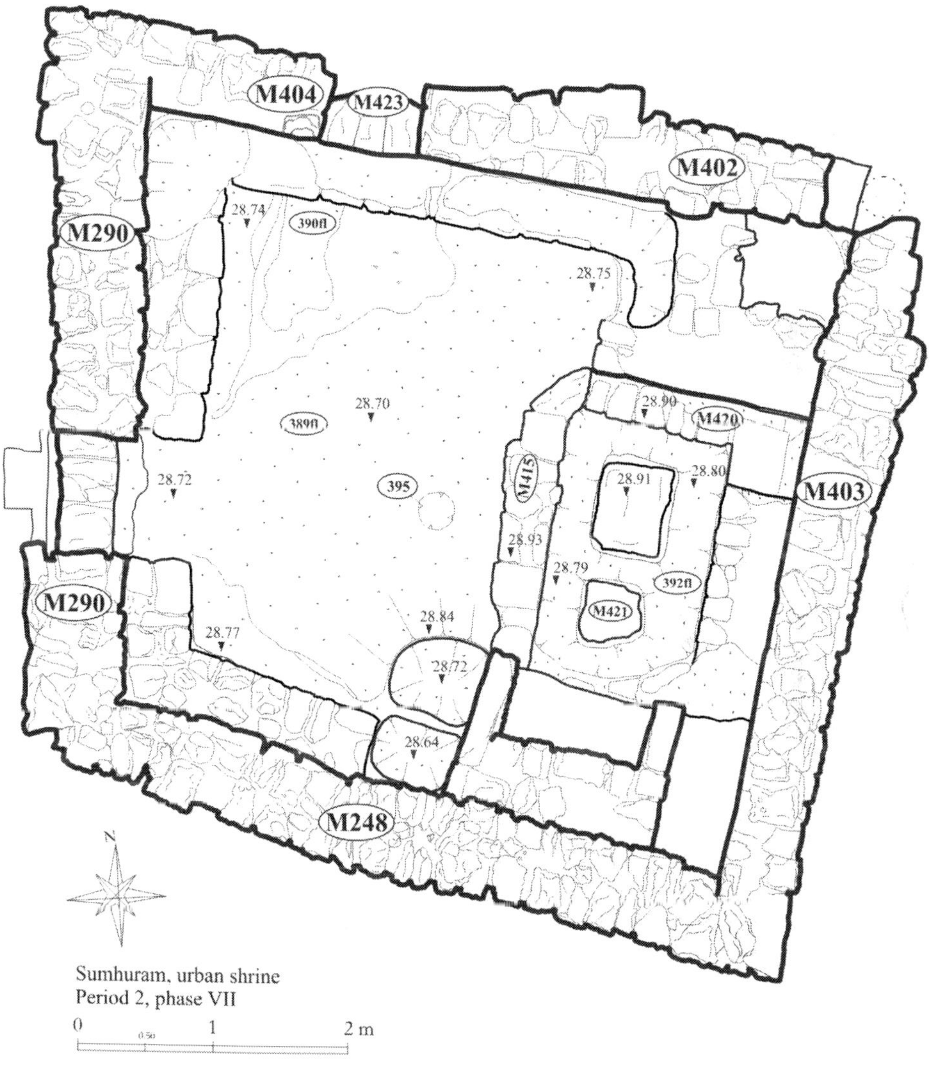

Plan of the shrine: Period II, Phase VII.

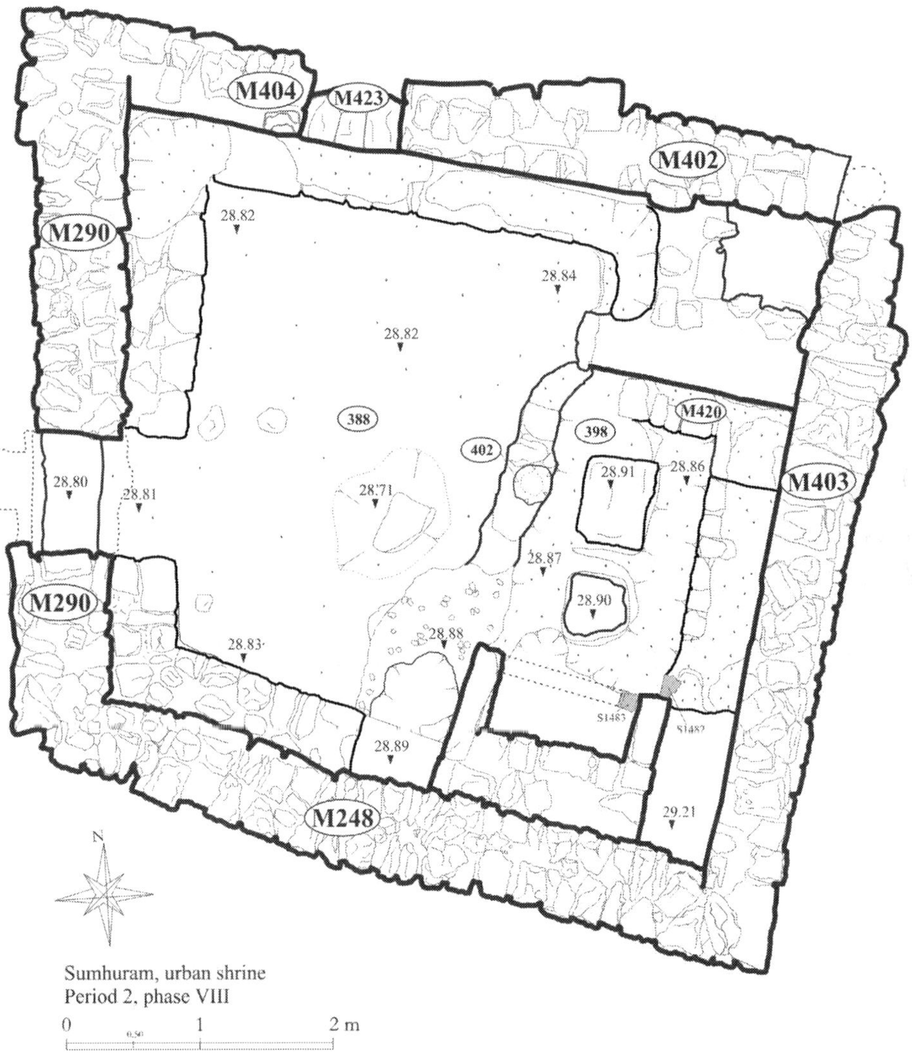

Plan of the shrine: Period 2, Phase VIII.

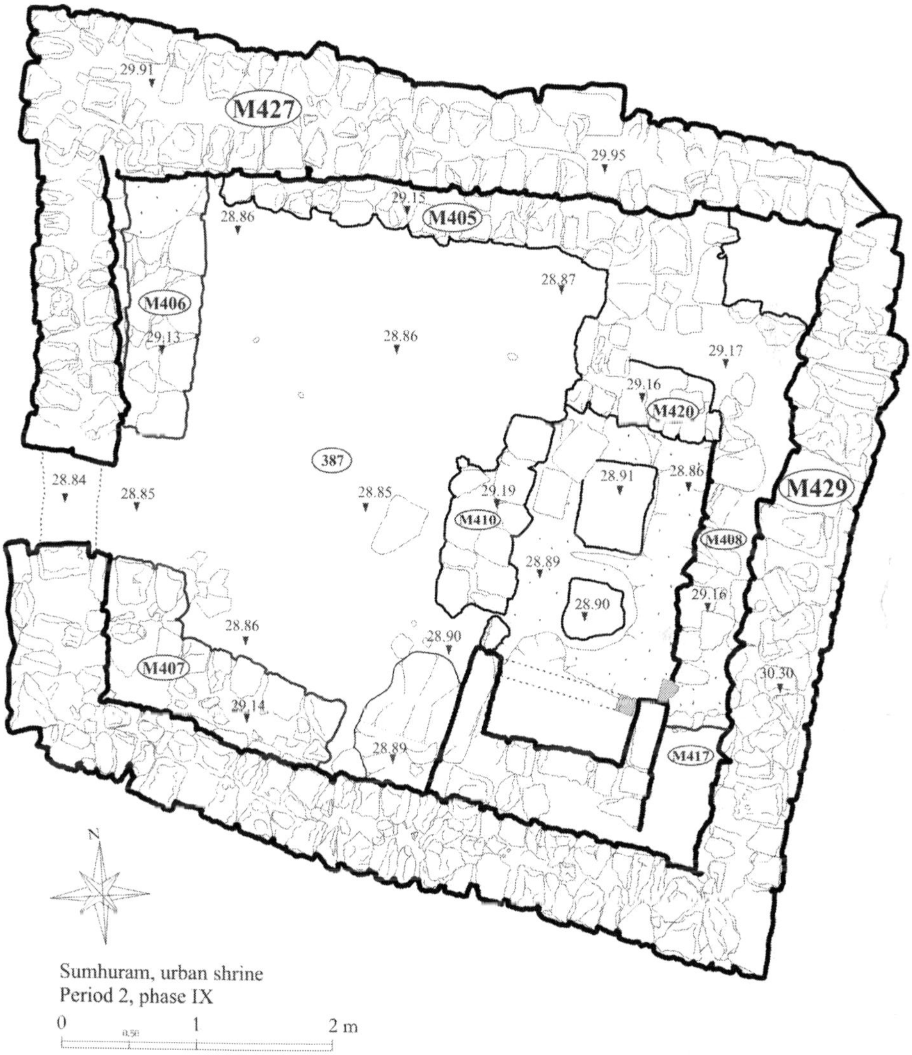

Plan of the shrine: Period II, Phase IX.

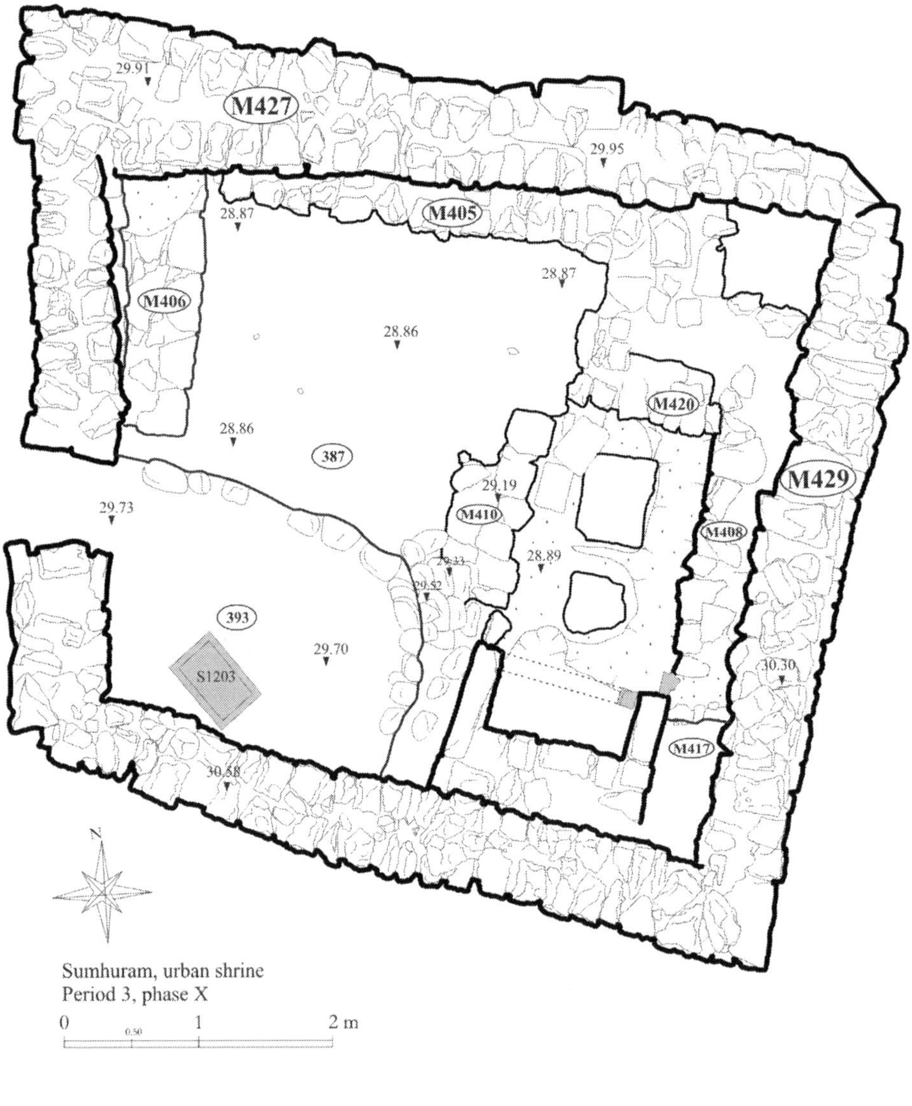

Plan of the shrine: Period 3, Phase X.

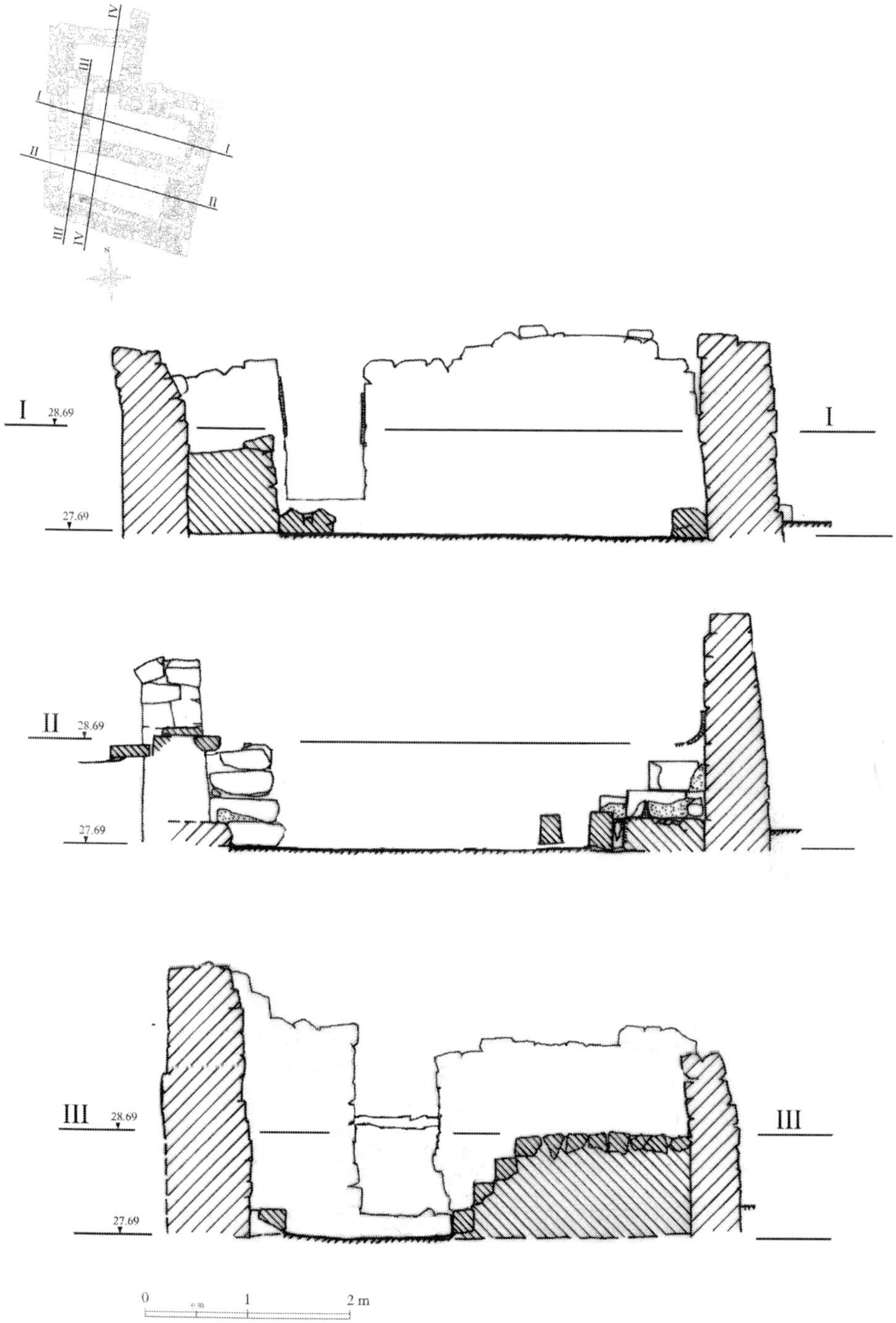

General sections of the shrine's main room (Period 1) and their location on the plan.

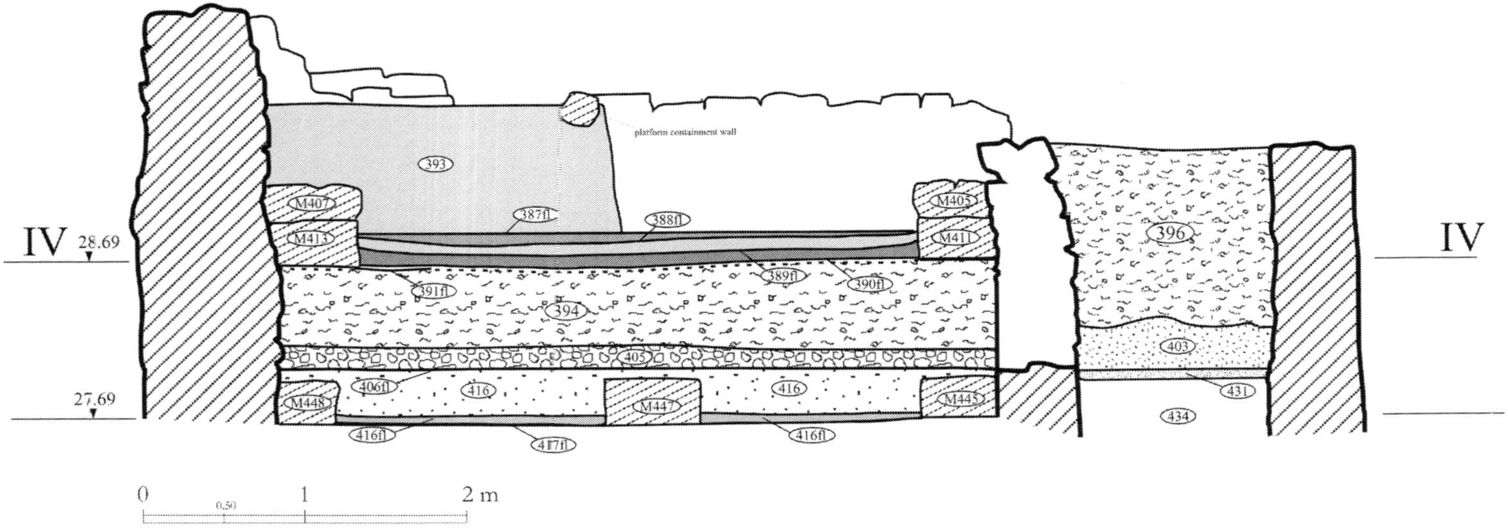

Stratigraphic section of the shrine, including annex Room A152. For location on the shrine's plan see Plate 11.

1

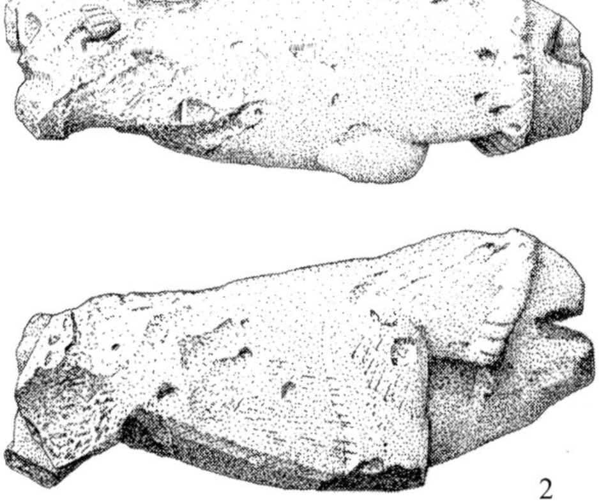

2

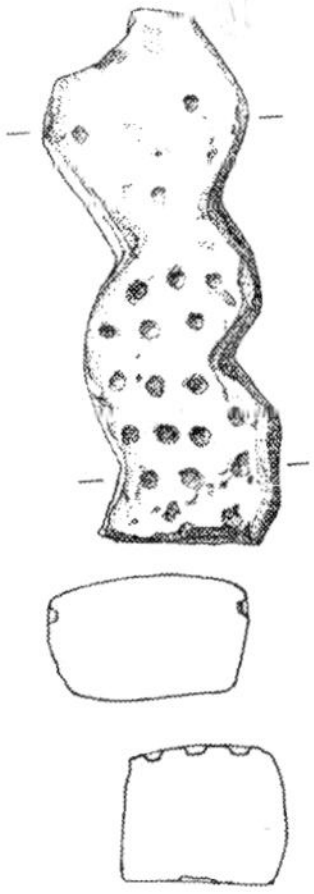

3

Stone statuary. 1: Head, cat. 1, S1193; 2: Lion statuette, cat. 2, S1194 (drawings by S. Martelli; scale 1:4). 3: Snake, cat. 3, S1529 (drawing by E. Kurkina; scale 1:3).

Bronze lion applique: cat. 4, MB625 (drawing by S. Martelli; scale 1:1).

Incense burner: cat. 8, S1197 (drawing by S. Martelli; scale 1:4).

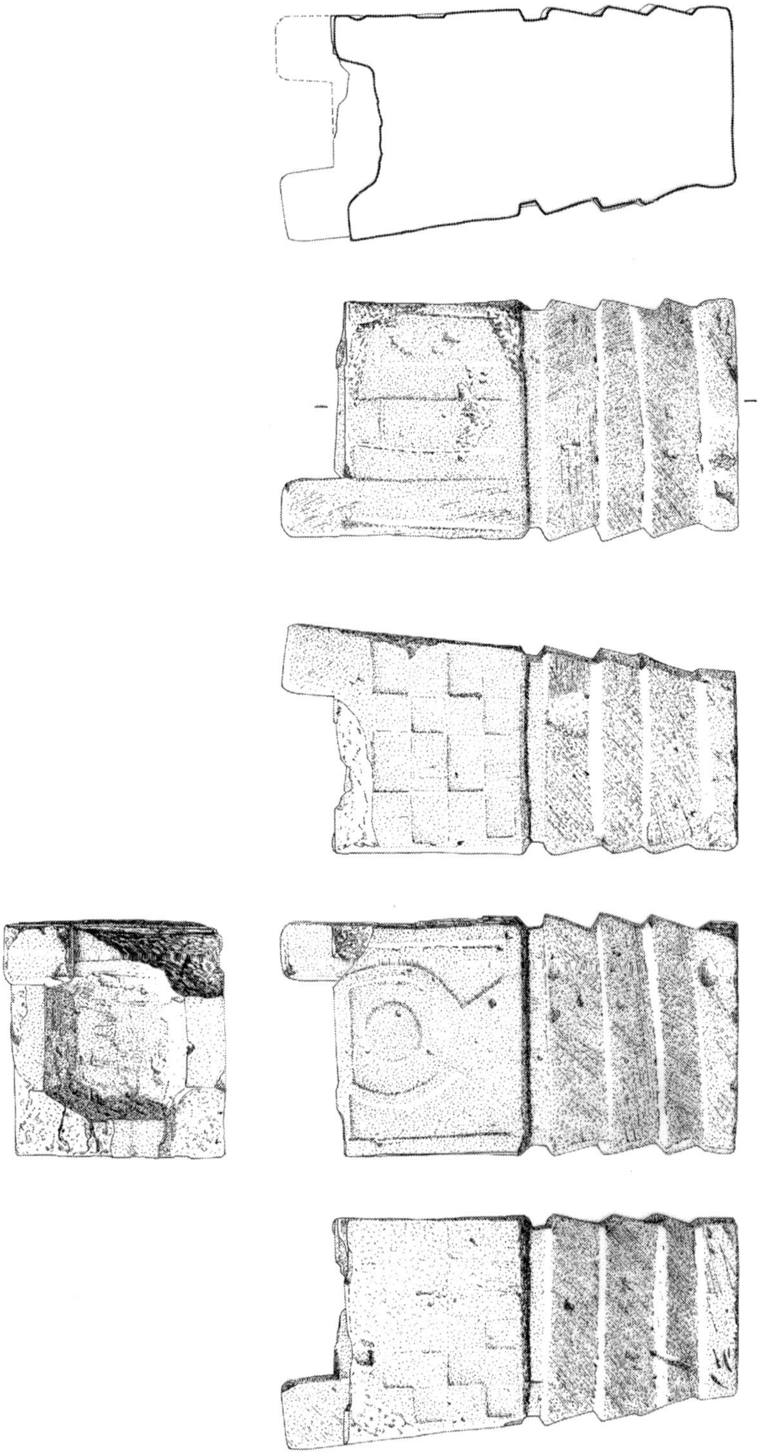

Incense burner: cat. 9, S1200 (drawing by S. Martelli; scale 1:5).

Incense burner: cat. 10, S1201 (drawing by S. Martelli; scale 1:5).

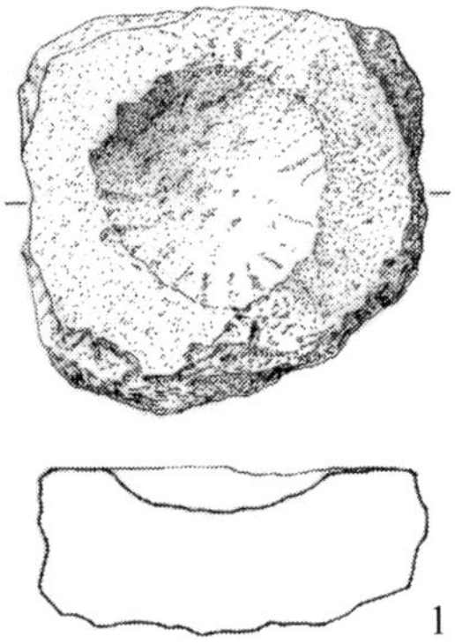

1

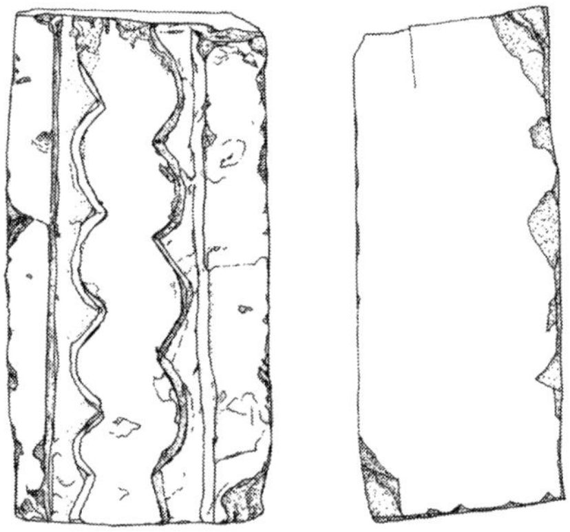

4

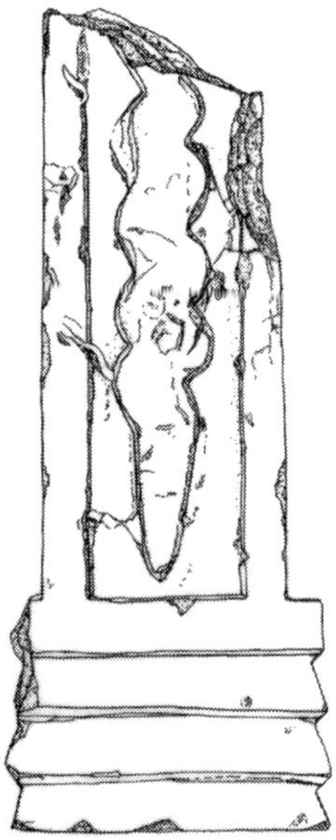

2

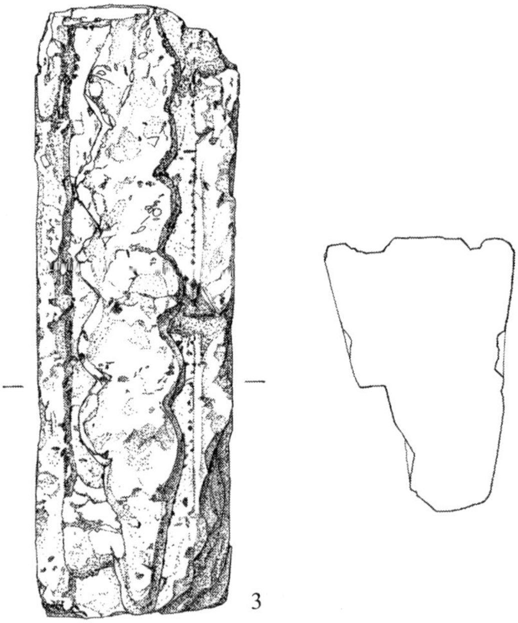

3

1: Incense burner, cat. 14, S1208 (drawing by S. Martelli; scale 1:4).
Architectural elements. 2: Pillar, cat. 17, S1494; 3: Pillar, cat. 18, S1495; 4: Pillar, cat. 19, S1539 (drawings by E. Kurkina; scale 1:5).

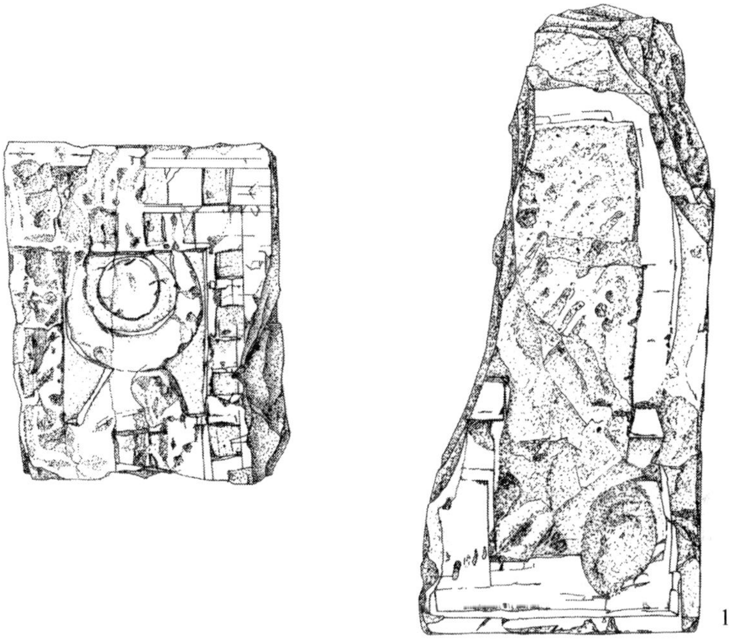

1

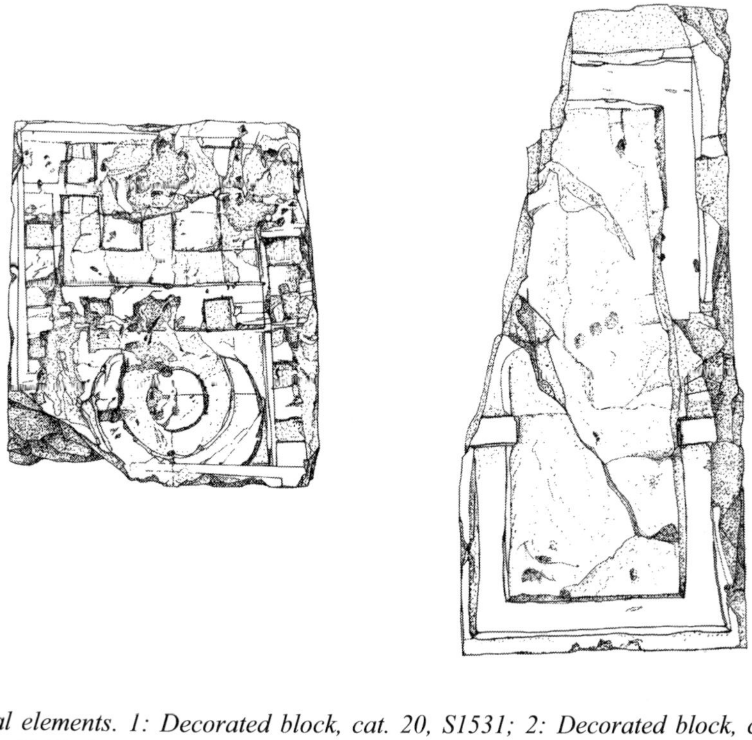

2

Architectural elements. 1: Decorated block, cat. 20, S1531; 2: Decorated block, cat. 21, S1532 (drawings by E. Kurkina; scale 1:5).

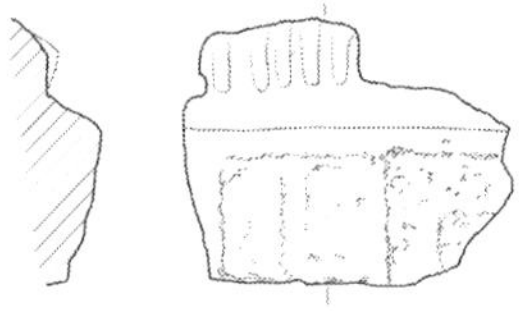
1

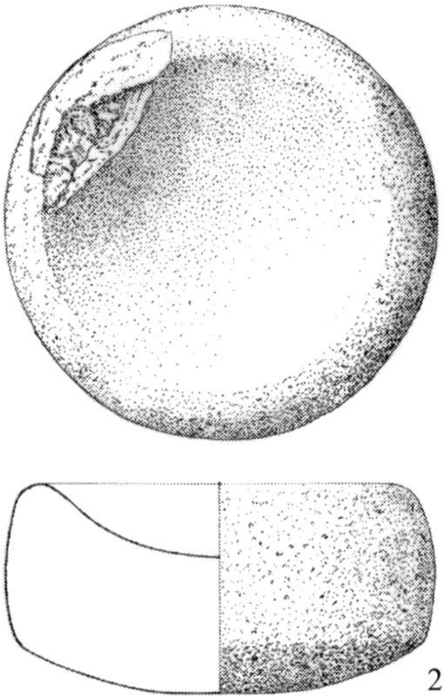
2

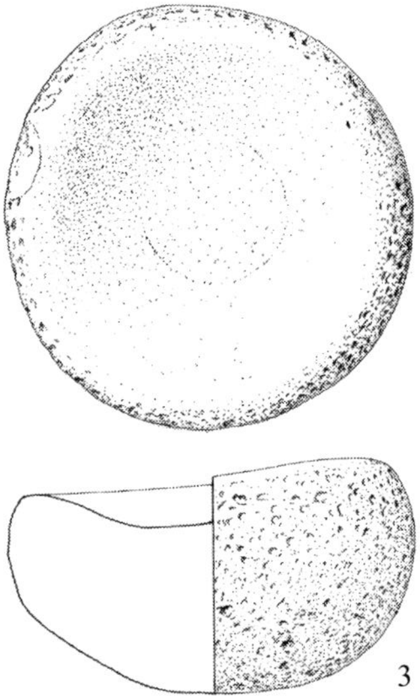
3

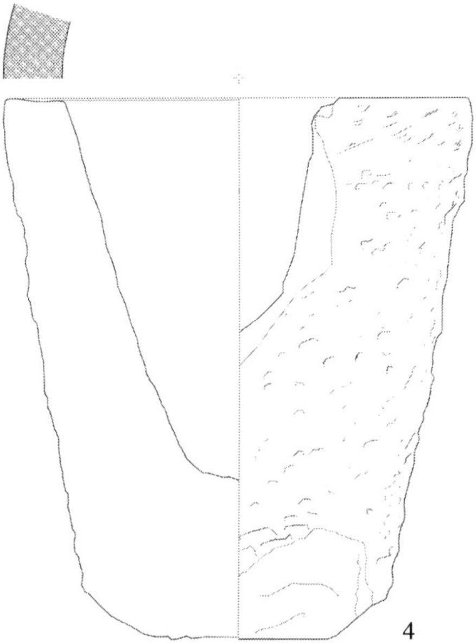
4

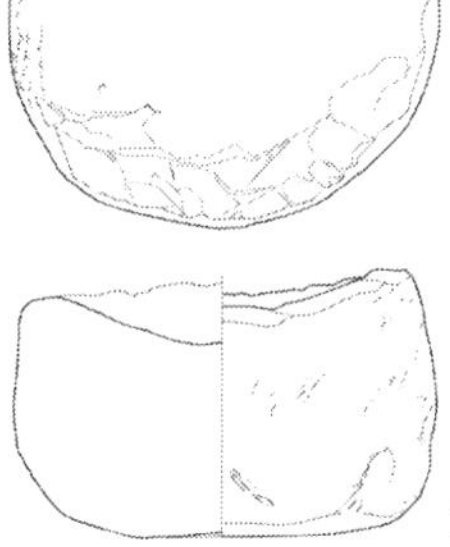
5

1: Architectural fragment, cat. 23, S1519 (drawing by S. Martelli; scale 1:3).
Stone tools. 2: Mortar, cat. 26, S1202; 3: Mortar, cat. 27, S1221; 4: Mortar, cat. 30, S1507; 5: Mortar, cat. 31, S1522 (drawings by S. Martelli; scale 1:4).

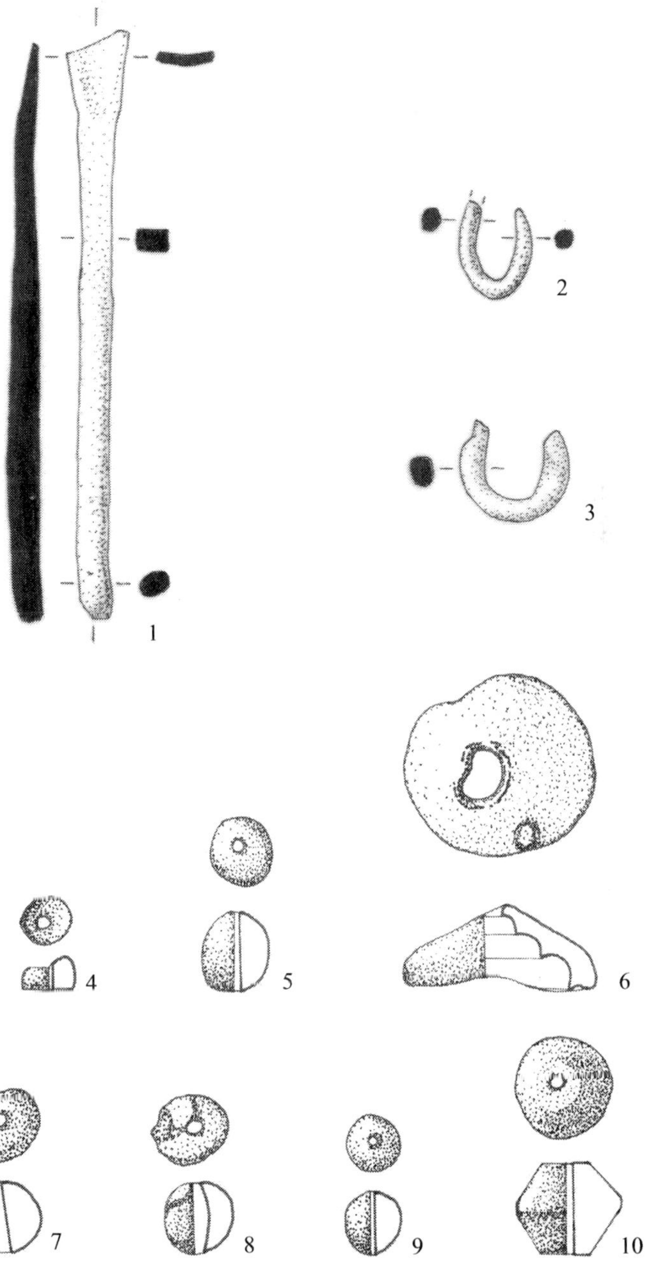

Personal adornments. 1: Bronze pin, cat. 38, MB604; 2: Bronze earring, cat. 39, MB526; 3: Bronze earring, cat. 40, MB528 (drawings by S. Martelli; scale 1:1).
Beads. 4: cat. 41, S1509; 5: cat. 42, S1526; 6: cat. 44, Sh358; 7: cat. 45, G140; 8: cat. 46, G141; 9: cat. 47, S1535; 10: cat. 48, S1501 (drawings by S. Lischi; scale 1.5:1).

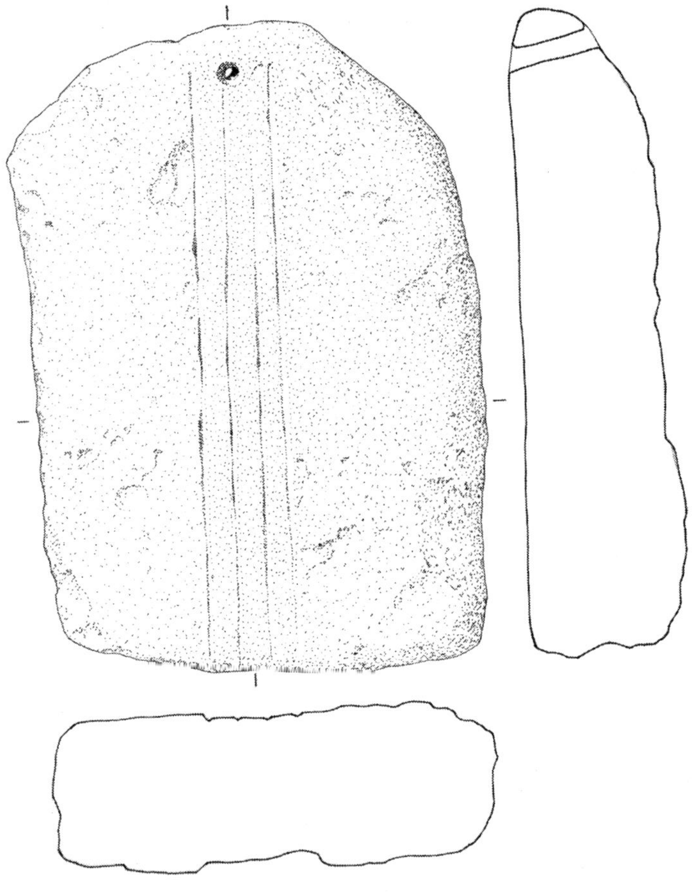

Pierced stone: cat. 50, S1196 (drawing by S. Martelli; scale 1:4).

1

2

3

Stone statuary. 1: Head, cat. 1, S1193; 2: Snake, cat. 3, S1529; 3: Lion statuette, cat. 2, S1194.

1

2

3

Templar Furnishing. 1: Basin, cat. 5, S1203; 2: Fragment of offering table, cat. 6, S1206; 3: Offering table, cat. 7, S1538.

1

2

3

Composite incense burners. 1: cat. 8, S1197; 2: cat. 9, S1200; 3: cat. 10, S1201.

1

2

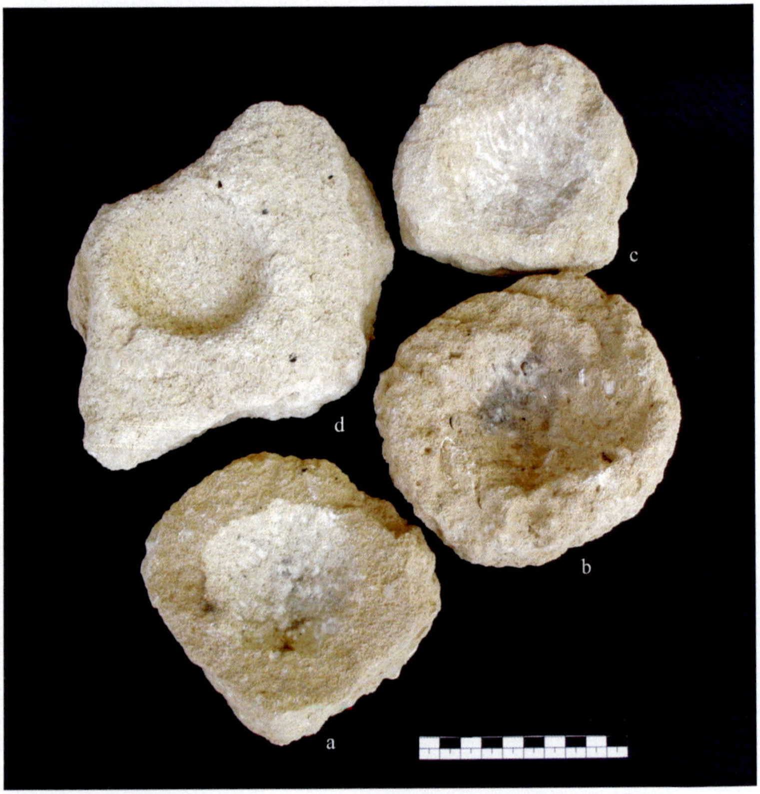

3

Incense burners. 1: cat.11, S1503; 2: cat. 12, 1504; 3a: cat. 13, S1207; 3b: cat. 15, S1209; 3c: cat. 14, S1208; 3d: cat. 16, S1218.

1

2

3

Architectural elements. 1: Pillar, cat. 17, S1494; 2: Pillar, cat. 18, S1495; 3 right: Decorated block, cat. 20, S1531; 3 left: Decorated block, cat. 21, S1532.

1

2

3

4

Architectural elements. 1: Lintel, cat. 22 , S1533; 2: High relief fragment, cat. 23, S1519; 3: Decorated block, cat. 24, S1514; 4: Architectural element, cat. 25, S1540.

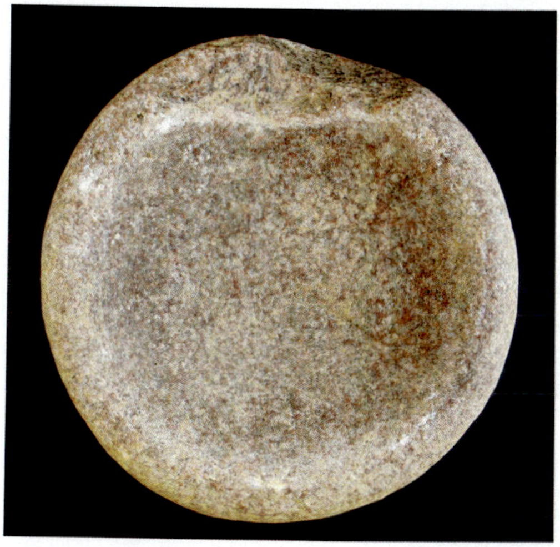

1

2

3

4

5

Stone tools - Mortars. 1: cat. 26, S1202; 2: cat. 27, S1221; 3: cat. 28, S1518; 4: cat. 29, S1224; 5: cat. 30, S1507.

Instrumenta. 1: Bronze handle, cat. 33, MB626; 2: Bone handle, cat. 34, B67; 3: Iron nail, cat. 35, MI159; 4: Iron nail, cat. 36, MI160; 5: Bronze plaque, cat. 37, MB605.

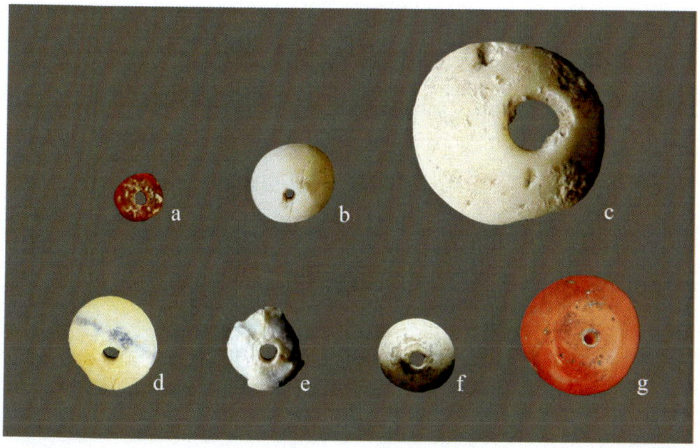

1

2

3

Beads. 1a: cat. 41, S1509; 1b: cat. 42, S1526; 1c: cat. 44, Sh358; 1d: cat. 45, G140; 1e: cat. 46, G141; 1f: cat. 47, S1535; 1g: cat. 48, S1501 (scale 1:5, except 1c: scale 1:1).
Varia. 2: Oil lamp, cat. 49, Sh359; 3: Dices, cat. 51, S1537.

Finito di stampare